'RACE', EDUCATION AND WORK:
THE STATISTICS OF INEQUALITY

Research in Ethnic Relations Series

Perceptions of Israeli Arabs: Territoriality and Identity
Izhak Schnell

Ethnic Mobilisation in a Multi-cultural Europe
Edited by John Rex and Beatrice Drury

Post-war Caribbean Migration to Britain:
The Unfinished Cycle
Margaret Byron

Through Different Eyes: The Cultural Identity of
Young Chinese People in Britain
David Parker

Britannia's Crescent: Making a Place for Muslims
in British Society
Danièle Joly

Religion, Class and Identity
The State, the Catholic Church and the Education
of the Irish in Britain
Mary J. Hickman

Migration, Citizenship and Ethno-National Identities
in the European Union
Edited by Marco Martiniello

Ethnic Conflict and Development: The Case of Guyana
Ralph R. Premdas

Ethnic Conflict and Development: The Case of Fiji
Ralph R. Premdas

'Race', Education and Work:
The Statistics of Inequality

DAVID DREW
Sheffield Hallam University

Avebury

Aldershot • Brookfield USA • Hong Kong • Singapore • Sydney

Published by
Avebury
Ashgate Publishing Limited
Gower House
Croft Road
Aldershot
Hants GU11 3HR
England

Ashgate Publishing Company
Old Post Road
Brookfield
Vermont 05036
USA

British Library Cataloguing in Publication Data

Drew, David
    'Race', Education and Work: Statistics of
    Inequality
    I. Title
    370.19342
ISBN 1 85972 111 7

Library of Congress Catalog Card Number: 95-78422

Printed and bound in Great Britain by
Ipswich Book Co. Ltd., Ipswich, Suffolk

Contents

Tables and figures

Chapter Three: Methodology

Tables

Figures

Chapter Four: Home and school at 16

Tables

Figures

Chapter Five: Post-compulsory education

Tables

Figures

Chapter Six: The youth labour market

Tables

Chapter Seven: Conclusion

Acknowledgements

I am indebted to a large number of people who helped me during the preparation of this book. I owe a large debt to my PhD supervisor, John Gray, for his guidance, encouragement and constructive criticism. He helped more than anyone to develop my thinking and to turn my raw ideas into something worthy of publication. He also encouraged me to keep writing when things got tough.

Acknowledgement needs to be made to the Department for Education and the Employment Department who funded the Youth Cohort Study and to the Nuffield Foundation which provided a small grant for an early part of the work. Particular thanks goes to the current project manager of the Youth Cohort Study, Gill Robson who has been very helpful in the latter stages of publication.

I am grateful for the support of all my colleagues in the Division of Education at the University of Sheffield and, in particular, those with whom I directly worked; Sean Demack, David Jesson, Shafeeq Ullhaq, Mark Tranmer, Charles Pattie and Nick Sime. A very big thank you goes to David Gillborn who read and commented on much of the draft and helped me considerably with my thinking about educational sociology. I am also grateful for support from the Division of Statistics and the Survey and Statistical Research Centre at Sheffield Hallam University, in particular Ashley Kershaw, Paresh Patel and Steve Wisher.

The ideas of a large number of people and their critical comments helped shape earlier drafts. For this, I'd like to thank Mike Atkins, Michael Banks, Dennis Brooks, Rachael Clarke, Elizabeth Clough, Bekia Fosam, Zahid Hamid, Jon Nixon, Eric Okell, Ian Plewis, Barry Troyna, Tony Wojciechowski, John Wrench and Cecile Wright. A particular thanks goes to John Bibby and Ludi Simpson who stayed at our house on a number of enjoyable occasions and had consistently good advice to give all along the way.

Jean Booker, Pauline Turner produced the text and the tables. A special thanks goes to them for their precision, patience and good humour. Gabrielle Turner composed the text during the final weeks and did a great job.

I am also indebted to many friends who have helped develop my political consciousness and have been supportive in other ways. I need to mention one particular friend, Ingo Gudjonsson. Ingo sustained me during highs and lows and without his help I would never have finished this.

Since this is my first single authored book (although hopefully not my last) I would like to pay tribute to a number of writers whose ideas have been an important influence.

The first of these is James Baldwin, whose book 'The Fire Next Time' was such a powerful indictment of the position of blacks in America in the sixties.

The second is C.L.R. James, the Afro-Caribbean historian whose book 'At the Rendezvous of Victory' showed that humour, sport and marxist writing could be combined.

The third is Nelson Mandela whose book 'No Easy Walk to Freedom' changed my world view on 'race' in the seventies.

The fourth is Chris Searle whose writing on politics and 'race' I greatly admire, whose work at Sheffield's Earl Marshal School has been inspirational and who encouraged me from the beginning to keep writing.

And the fifth is Barry Troyna, a prolific writer on racism and anti-racism in education who encouraged me to do statistical research on 'race' and showed me that coming from a North London working class background and supporting Tottenham Hotspur FC (which I did in my youth) were quite good credentials for entry to the field of educational sociology.

I also want to express my gratitude to my family. To Lucy and James Jack, (latterly coxswain of the Anstruther lifeboat), who introduced me to the wonderful world of fishermen in the East Neuk of Fife and showed a continuing interest in all my projects. To my parents who made many things possible. To our children, Rachel and Sarah who have acted with great patience when I couldn't play with them. And to Fiona Jack who has too many good qualities to mention.

Finally if this book were to be dedicated to a group of people it would be to the group of undergraduates that I taught in 1970 at the

University of Sierre Leone many of whom went on to great things. They were superb students who mixed humour with brilliance and showed me, inexperienced as I was, how to party.

Dedicated to the future of.....

Rachel and Sarah

Dedicated to the memory of .....

Samora Machel and Cathie Marsh

No race holds the monopoly of beauty, of intelligence, of strength and there is a place for all at the rendezvous of victory.

Aimé Cesaire, Return to My Native Land
(Cahier d`un retour au pays natal)

1 Introduction

This book is a statistical analysis of the 'race', gender and social class differences in educational attainment and progress into jobs of 28,000 black and white young people aged 16-19, charted through the Youth Cohort Study of England and Wales. But it is about much more than that. It is about the individual struggles of Afro-Caribbean and Asian young people, to improve their life chances in a job market characterised both by recession and racial discrimination. And it is important not to lose sight of the individuals themselves within the statistics that follow within these pages.

To a certain extent the struggles of ethnic minority young people are no different from those of their white counterparts. The problems of obtaining appropriate level qualifications and choosing the best route through education into jobs is, to some extent, independent of ethnic background. But the labour market itself is very different for ethnic minority young people because of the racial discrimination that pervades it, despite twenty years of race relations legislation (Brown, 1992). It is the innovative and imaginative ways in which ethnic minority young people are attempting to overcome such problems that are of particular interest, representing as they almost always do a second or third generation of ethnic minorities in England and Wales. Their parents or grandparents may have been immigrants to Britain but this group has practically all been born and educated here. If their schooling does not adequately prepare them for the world of work, then it is the schools of England and Wales that are, at least in part, responsible.

Since research continues to show the persistent effects of racial discrimination in the labour market, it would be tempting to frame an analysis of this kind in terms of Afro-Caribbean and Asian young people as victims of a racist society and the attempts of individuals to overcome bias and prejudice, whether in the classroom or in the world at large. Such an approach has strong merit and some research (see, for example Mac an Ghail, 1989) has analysed school processes and the resistance of Afro-Caribbean and Asian young people using such a framework with a qualitative research methodology. This approach has not, however been very explicit in the more statistical approaches to the area, which in a sense is surprising given that statistical analysis lends itself to the study of inequality. It should be possible to detect the effects of discriminatory processes by careful statistical analysis. This is the approach used in this book always bearing in mind that ethnic minority young people experience racism in different ways and to different degrees and therefore we cannot assume that their experiences will be similar.

The differences in the way people experience racism in their every day lives has been used in a perverse way by critics to deny that such racism exists. By pointing to individuals who have succeeded despite having a brown skin the suggestion is made that everyone has the opportunity to succeed by similar hard work. Even the most casual analysis of the statistical data of the last 30 years, however shows this argument to be dubious and it is the purpose of this book to add to a statistical understanding of this process, by analysis of the largest statistical data set on the topic to date.

It might also be tempting, at least if research up to the Swann Report in 1985 (Department of Education and Science, 1985) was used as a model, to use quite another approach and to frame an analysis in terms of ethnic minority 'underachievement'. Such an analysis might focus on average differences in attainment and high unemployment levels and explain them in terms of a deficit model, that is the failure of individuals to succeed within the education system with a consequent and predictable failure within the labour market.

At its most extreme this model was postulated in the 'race' and IQ debate which suggests that blacks are innately and genetically inferior to whites and that their intellectual progress will necessarily be limited, whatever resources are devoted to their education. Such arguments have a history dating back at least to the beginning of the nineteenth century in Britain and elsewhere and they have never been successfully sustained by detailed statistical analysis, despite determined attempts to do so (see the critique in Gill and Levidow, 1987). There has, in the United States been a surprising but not totally

2

unexpected revival of such views with the publication by Herrnstein and Murray of 'The Bell Curve' in 1994 (Herrnstein and Murray, 1994). Not only does the book claim that extra funds provided to educate blacks is ill spent but it claims that the best way forward is for wealthy white families to adopt black children. This book has sold over 500,000 copies in the US. which shows that there is considerable interest in such views there still, despite the fact that the book is based largely on old ideas and recycled data.

The analysis in my book is not based on the deficit or underachievement model and it has been the purpose of this research to contribute to a sound statistical reinterpretation of the data on ethnic minority achievement in education (see, for example the critique by Troyna, 1984).

In statistical analyses we often make the point that variability (variance) is just as important as the average (mean) and in this book too it is the diversity of experience that is important as well as the generalizations we might make about groups. This study is a tribute to ethnic minority young people and the diverse strategies that they have adopted to solve their educational and job problems.

Parts of this study have already been published elsewhere (see Drew and Gray, 1990; Drew and Gray, 1991; Drew, Gray and Sime, 1992 and Drew, 1993). It covers the period of the mid to late eighties. In 1984 the older members of the study were 16 years old and were at an age when they were free to leave education permanently if they so wished. In 1989 the younger members of the study had reached 19 years of age.

What were the factors affecting ethnic minority young people during this period? (In this study the term black is sometimes, though rarely, used to describe people of Afro-Caribbean and Asian origin and a discussion of this terminology is given in Chapter three.) How were they responding to these? In what ways did the circumstances of ethnic minority and white young people differ? What changes were taking place in education and the youth labour market at this time?

The best starting point for the answer to these questions lies with the young people themselves. There was a feeling of anger, particularly amongst those who could not find a job. An Afro-Caribbean interviewee quoted in Scott (1990: 24) said the following:

> There has been many a time when I phoned up for an application form for a job in my best Birmingham accent. My name is Smith so they obviously thought I was white, and they told me to come along so that they could talk to me. As soon as I got there it was

3

obvious they weren't expecting a black person and they made excuses why they didn't want me. They're the sort of people who don't believe you when you say you were born in Birmingham.

This anger was not simply the frustration of a college leaver not being able to get a job, it was also an anger about the difference it made being black. Young people make decisions as they enter the labour market, based on the evidence available to them. The evidence is that racism is a major factor in their lives at school and in the transition from school to work. This may take the form of racial harassment in the playground, the experience of racist attitudes from certain teachers and direct and indirect discrimination by training scheme managers and employers.

The conclusion that racism is such an important factor in the experience of Afro-Caribbean and Asian young people in the 1980s is not one derived simply from an inspection of current empirical data. There is a long history of racism in Britain and this has had its effect on the whole population of Britain, whatever their ethnic background. The slave trade and the expansion of the British Empire not only illustrate the reasons for the geographical movements of labour from Africa to the Caribbean and hence to Britain but are also linked with the development of racist attitudes amongst white English people.

This study is about the world of education and the world of work. As far as ethnic minority young people are concerned these worlds have, during the past decade, been affected by responses at government and local level.

The education context

The education system has, during the last thirty years been slow to respond to the needs of black and ethnic minorities people. There have been, it has been argued, three broad phases in the policy responses by government over this period; assimilation, integration and cultural pluralism (Troyna, 1992).

Up until the sixties in Britain, ethnic minorities were seen largely as immigrants who needed to become assimilated into the British way of life. This was inevitably to be a one way process, ethnic minorities people were being encouraged to become similar to whites. The focus in education therefore was on the linguistic needs of the newly arrived ethnic minorities and the teaching of English as a second language. There was also the much more dubious policy of the dispersal of

4

ethnic minority pupils to different schools by 'bussing', based on the assumption that too many such pupils in one school would have a bad effect on the progress of white pupils.

In the late sixties the focus changed to integration. This, according to Roy Jenkins, the Home Secretary in 1966, referred not to a 'flattening process of assimilation' but to 'equal opportunity accompanied by cultural diversity, in an atmosphere of mutual tolerance' (Troyna, 1992: 68). There were a number of aspects to this multicultural approach. There was an emphasis on learning about the culture and traditions of ethnic minorities firstly to reduce (white) children's prejudice towards those of different cultures and secondly to improve (ethnic minority) children's educational achievement and to create equality of opportunity.

The supposed educational underachievement of Afro-Caribbean children led to the Committee of Enquiry under Rampton which finally reported under Lord Swann in 1985 (DES, 1985). This report reflected the third phase, that of cultural pluralism. By this time an argument was being made that it was not simply educational attainment that needed scrutiny. Wider issues required attention; the extent to which teachers attitudes and expectations affected ethnic minority children, (Middleton, 1983) the importance of a curriculum that would reflect a multicultural society (Tomlinson, 1987) and the particular problems of racial bullying and harassment in the classroom and playground. This wider set of issues included racism in the school, amongst teachers and in society in general. There was considerable disagreement at this stage between those whose main focus was on prejudice as an individual problem (the 'multicultural' approach) and those who wished to focus on more structural issues and the way in which racism helps maintain injustice in society (the 'anti-racist' approach).

The Swann report added to this debate. It was the first government report to mention racism (even though its chairman in a lengthy separate summary did not use the word once). In its terms of reference the assertion was made that the educational performance of ethnic minority children was influenced by three sets of factors; those factors indigenous to the educational system, the economic prospects of school leavers and influences in early childhood. These terms of reference provided fuel for those coming from different polarised educational positions and the difficulties, conflicts and contradictions faced by the Committee are reflected in its report. (For a discussion of these conflicts by one of the Committee's members, see Parekh, 1992 and for a critique of the political roles of such Committees see Gurnah, 1987).

The report is wide ranging. Such was the need to cover all possible reactions to its findings that the Committee even saw it necessary to return to the old IQ debate, the question of the alleged genetic inferiority of Afro-Caribbean children. It commissioned two Cambridge academics to deal with this in a lengthy paper. In the end there was no clear conclusion reached about underachievement, the report balanced the arguments of both the 'multicultural' and 'anti-racist' positions. But the report was very influential in the way this and other issues were debated. In the first place it gave serious and thoughtful consideration to racism as both an individual and structural phenomenon (see Gillborn, 1990). In the second place it discussed curriculum materials and the attitudes which condition the selection of subject matter and which underlie the teaching process. In the third place it showed concern about the 'hidden curriculum', the unstated norms and values transmitted to students.

The response of government to the report was disappointing. The Swann Committee presented a range of recommendations but important parts were immediately rejected. Three years later the 1988 Education Reform Act set up a national curriculum for schools and in the Act there was little mention of the need for a curriculum that reflected the multicultural nature of British society. Multicultural issues were marginalized as a 'cross-curricular dimension' (Hardy and Vieler-Porter, 1992).

The response to the Swann report at the local authority level has been less disappointing but fraught with problems. In Brent, for example, a Development Programme for Race Equality was set up in 1986 which devoted considerable resources to a plan for curriculum change, staff development and organizational development. These proposals were widely and savagely attacked in the press, particularly the proposals for coordinators in the schools ('Race Spies Shock', the Mail on Sunday). The programme was eventually wound up in 1990. Those most deeply involved were critical of political and policy mistakes that were made in the implementation of the plan (see Richardson, 1992) and these criticisms were echoed by others involved in race equality initiatives in other authorities (see Ouseley, 1992).

In retrospect there has been a re-evaluation of the debate about 'multicultural' and 'anti-racist' approaches in education and there has been a tendency for some writers who adopt an anti-racist position to

6

see weaknesses in the way anti-racist policies were formulated and put into practice (see Troyna, 1992).

The employment context

In employment, the problems faced by young people entering work for the first time were an increase in unemployment and, for ethnic minority young people, continuing discrimination in the labour market. The responses at government level had been mixed. Shortages of labour led to moves to encourage immigration into Britain in the fifties and sixties but this additional source of labour supply was, by the seventies, no longer needed. Successive immigration acts culminating in the 1981 Nationality Act had successfully restricted immigration. In parallel, the 1976 Race Relations Act had attempted to address the problem of discrimination in employment and other fields. Whilst the declared intentions of the Act were impressive; that discrimination should be unlawful where it occurs in the offering of work, terms and conditions, promotion, training, benefits services and facilities and dismissal, the reality was less convincing. The number of tribunal proceedings for individual complaints of discrimination was exceedingly small relative to the number of cases of discrimination which it was estimated were taking place (Ohri and Faruqi in Bhat et al, 1988). It was difficult in these cases to obtain evidence to show discrimination and the compensation awarded in successful cases was small. Furthermore the CRE had been able only to make restricted use of its power to carry out formal investigations of employers and the effectiveness of such investigations had been limited. The CRE's proposals for amendments of the Act (CRE, 1986) had met with a muted response from government.

If recourse to the law seemed to have only limited value, the other direction from which change was coming was from the equal opportunity policies of employers, predominantly those in the public sector. Whilst, under the 1976 Race Relations Act it was unlawful to discriminate in favour of someone on the grounds that such a person had been discriminated against in the past, the Act did permit some positive action. The CRE attempted to encourage this through a Code of Practice on Employment. There was, though, a large difference between policy and practice; between having an equal opportunities statement and actually implementing it. The declared intention not to discriminate was common compared with the implementation of fair recruitment practices with a measurable impact on the labour force which was far more rare. The Greater London Council was one of a small number of local authorities which put policy into practice (Drew, 1986). The GLC was a large employer in a city with a sizeable ethnic minority population and this population was significantly under represented in its work force. The GLC implemented in the early eighties a system of equality targets supported by a system of personnel planning and recruitment monitoring. As a result the percentage of Afro-Caribbean and Asian men and women in the work force increased at a dramatic rate, in one year (1981) by fifty per cent. Ethnic minority staff increased from an estimated 8 per cent in 1978 to a quarter in 1985. Such policies were pursued not only in London (for example in Hackney and Lambeth see Ouseley, 1982) but elsewhere (for example in Bradford and Leicester).

The impact of these policies in some authorities was strongly felt. Local authorities were generally large employers in their own area and it was apparent that ethnic minority people were under represented in the labour force in general and in the higher administrative and professional grades in particular. Positive action policies revised priorities in favour of these groups.

The effects of these policies should not be overstated, however. They were not an unqualified success. In the first place their numerical impact was not always great. Their effectiveness was often measured more in terms of inputs - the number of race advisers, their status, the level of grant provided to ethnic minority groups, than outputs - the number of ethnic minority people who benefited and the introduction of fairer policies. Conflict was bound to result from the challenge to existing power structures but this was, according to critics, (see Lansley, Goss and Wolmar, 1989) compounded by inadequacies in implementation, a confusion about what such policies could or should achieve (equality of opportunity or equality of outcome), an excessive emphasis on tackling individual instead of institutional racism and an underestimation of the nature and pervasiveness of racism itself (see Gilroy, 1992). A start though had been made and large companies in the private sector had begun to adopt some of the policies (for example, ethnic monitoring), that had been shown to be useful, even though their progress in this direction was slow (see Gibbon, 1990 and Jewson et al, 1992 for empirical studies of this and Young, 1992 for a discussion of policy development in this field).

The effects of such changes on black young people were therefore mixed. In some areas and in some cities black young people might be aware that some attention was being paid by employers to the

8

particular problems they faced in finding jobs. But overall the effects were slight. Of much greater importance to them was the rise in general levels of unemployment as a result of which job opportunities for young people in general and black young people in particular had become much more scarce.

Economic policies had contributed to a decline in manufacturing industries and a major recession at the beginning of the Eighties with high youth unemployment as a result. The Youth Training Scheme had grown out of this. The structure of the scheme passed through a number of phases during this study; in 1984 it was a one year scheme and it was extended to a two year scheme in 1986. By the end of the decade the provision of training had been devolved to the newly created Training and Enterprise Councils (TECs) set up in local areas. Youth Training was presented as a major improvement in the provision of vocational training for young people in parallel with systems in other European countries. Germany was held up as a model for a comprehensive system of post-16 training. In Britain, however a variety of criticisms were made; young people frequently saw schemes as providing inadequate training at a low wage and the quality of schemes was seen to be highly variable.

By the mid eighties the Youth Training Scheme, whatever its limitations, was in place as one of the major routes into the youth labour market, particularly for those with moderate or relatively few qualifications at 16. About one third of all young people followed this route. In planning both YTS and its predecessor, the Youth Opportunities Programme, the Training Agency made a clear commitment to declare and implement an equal opportunities policy in the administration of schemes. Since YTS represented large scale government intervention in the labour market it might have been seen as a major opportunity for government to prevent the racism present in the labour market in general being reflected in post-compulsory education and training. This opportunity seems to have been lost. There were already fears by the early eighties that ethnic minority young people were concentrated in schemes where they were least likely to find work on completion of their training (Fenton et al, 1984). And other research showed both covert resistance and blatant racism on the part of YTS employers and sponsors (Cross and Wrench, 1991: 27).

9

Gender and social class

There are, in summary, a variety of contexts that provide the backdrop to this study. They can be summarized simply by saying that, wherever you look at education, youth training or the labour market, being a member of an ethnic minority group makes a difference. It makes a difference in teacher attitudes, relationships with other pupils, attainment in examinations, the decision to stay on in further and higher education, YTS participation, applying for jobs and the outcome of the job search. What is also apparent is that other factors make a considerable difference also.

Equality of opportunity for women also is at issue here. Gender differences are apparent in almost all the above areas. There has been the development, parallel to race relations legislation, of gender related legislation on employment and discrimination. The parallel here is that, whilst equality of opportunity for women has become embodied in law, there are many who would argue that changes in practice have not kept pace with changes in legislation. Many women are still concentrated in part-time, low paid, semi-skilled occupations and in the small number of professional occupations in which numerically women play a large part (for example nursing and teaching) their advancement is slower than that of their male counterparts. For similar levels of qualifications and experience they are lower paid than men. (For a study of gender differences amongst nurses see Drew, Okell and Wisher, 1988 and for a study of gender differences in teachers' pay, albeit in a US context, see Lee and Smith 1989. Both studies used statistical procedures to control for qualifications and experience in order to make comparisons between males and females).

The social class differences in education in Britain have been well documented over the decades of the post-war period. They affect the home background of young people and influence attitudes and experiences from an early age (Tizard et al, 1988). In the post-war period the numbers of working class children proceeding to post-compulsory and higher education and the professions has increased (see Heath, 1981) but at a rather slow rate. This particular aspect of British society has been somewhat resistant to change. Social class differences persist in education and are evidenced in the jobs which working class young people expect and obtain (Willis, 1977). The connection between this and the experiences of ethnic minority young people is, however, not an easy one. Ethnic minority young people become part of a class differentiated system in which they or their parents or grandparents are relative newcomers and therefore they are likely to experience these differences in a somewhat different way from those with a longer history of living here and a longer familiarity with this country's institutions.

These factors add a complexity which it is important to explore. A young woman whose parents emigrated to Britain from a rural area of Bangladesh, whose father was employed in a steelworks in Sheffield in an unskilled job until being made redundant has a very different background to a young woman whose parents originally came from Goa in Southern India, who was born and brought up in Uganda where her father was an entrepreneur and manager, who attended a private school there and who subsequently came to Britain when the Asians were expelled by Amin. Both women might be classified as 'Asian females' in a statistical study and yet their backgrounds are worlds apart.

The two examples are factual. The first woman was living in Sheffield, the second in Edgware, North London. The areas in which they lived also affected their employment prospects. Take Sheffield, for example. The local labour market there was heavily dependent until the early eighties on manufacturing industry in general and the steel industry in particular. The semi-skilled and skilled work force was drawn from the established working class area of east Sheffield, (Attercliffe, Burngreave and Darnall) and the large local authority housing estates. Into these areas, at a time when there was a shortage of labour supply, moved a small group of Bangladeshi men who were later to be joined by their families. The collapse of the steel industry in the eighties led to high levels of unemployment in these areas and especially within the Bangladeshi community. The local labour market in North London was, by contrast, buoyant in the eighties and unemployment was low relative to other parts of England and Wales.

Whilst the factors of gender, social class and the local labour market differentiate ethnic minorities there remains the common factor of racism which all ethnic minority young people experience. In the next section this issue will be addressed.

Racism

There are very different approaches to the notion of racism. It is useful here to briefly review some of the major developments. The debate is a complex one. A model is a 'device which reduces the complexity of what is represented, by selectively reproducing only

11

those details which are deemed significant or useful for the purpose at hand' (Cohen, 1992: 63). All such models are therefore only a partial view of reality.

The term pseudo-scientific racism has been given to the theory in the nineteenth century that distinctive human characteristics and abilities were determined by 'race'. This was based on the hypothesis that there was a hierarchy of biologically distinct groups and that 'races' (for example Caucasian, Mongoloid and Negroid) could be described as superior or inferior relative to each other. A number of different attempts were made by biologists to justify this hierarchy of groups. These included attempts to classify the shapes of skulls (craniology) and to predict individuals characteristics from the contours of their skulls (phrenology, see Fryer, 1987).

Phrenologists believed that there was a correlation between the shape of the head in different human groups and their degree of civilisation. Africans were inferior to Europeans, as were Hindus. Phrenology was used to justify empire-building. It told the British that they were ruling over races that, unlike themselves, lacked force of character (for an analysis of how Europe 'underdeveloped' Africa see Rodney, 1972).

These classifications (see Miles, 1989) broke down under the weight of logical inconsistency and empirical evidence and the theories became discredited. It took much longer for the ideas to recede from popular use however (see Benedict, 1983) and the terminology (Caucasian etc.) was until recently still used in ethnic categories by the Metropolitan Police.

A second explanatory model is that of institutional racism. Influential in this was the book by Stokely Carmichael and Charles Hamilton (1968) in the United States at the time of the emergence of the Black Power Movement. Their definition included all those beliefs, actions and processes (whether intentional or not) which led to or sustained discrimination against or subordination of black people. This drew attention to the cumulative effects of individual acts of prejudice and discrimination within organisations and institutions and to structures which, deliberate or not, had the effect of disadvantaging black people (see, for example, Sivanandan, 1982). Explicit motive or intention was not a necessary condition for an activity to be described as institutional racism. This emphasis on consequences rather than intentional action was criticised, particularly in Britain. The broadness of this definition was described as 'conceptual inflation' by Miles (1989). (See also Troyna and Williams, 1986).

This discussion reflects the continuing debate in Britain about neo-Marxist and neo-Weberian models of 'race' and racism. Marxist models (see Castles and Kosack, 1973) place emphasis on the nature of capitalism and the role of immigrants in the supply of labour and the class structure. This was adapted in the neo-Marxist approach which avoided the economic determinism and reductionism of traditional Marxism. This approach is particularly associated with writers at the Centre for Contemporary Cultural Studies (see CCCS, 1982; Gilroy, 1987 and a discussion of developments in this area by Solomos, 1986). They argue that there is not one single definition of racism but a number of historically specific racisms and that racism is a continually changing phenomena. They also reject a clear dichotomy between 'race' and class and argue that it is impossible to understand either through separate analysis of the two.

Complementary to the neo-Marxist models are the neo-Weberian models (see Rex and Moore, 1967; Rex, 1973; Rex and Mason, 1986). In 'Race, Community and Conflict' published in 1967, Rex and Moore elaborated on the idea that competition over housing was central to the competitive process for ethnic groups and they introduced the concept of housing classes. This Weberian approach was reformulated in later publications. By 1986 Rex was suggesting that an underclass of immigrants existed in British society, a quasi-group with a distinct class position and status, weaker and lower than that of the working class.

Recently, these models have been increasingly criticised. 'The problems with all these formulations is that they are reductionist: that is, they claim that complex and multi-faceted phenomena can be explained by a single, simple cause. These explanations are therefore limited' (Cohen, 1992). They argue that a wider view should be taken of racism and ethnicity (see Hall, 1992a, 1992b and 1992c). The same issue is taken up by Modood (1992). He is especially keen to break down thinking along the lines of 'racial dualism' categorising everyone as either white or black and believes there has been an overemphasis on 'colour racism' at the expense of concern about 'cultural racism' which is a different but related issue. While racism remains a critical concern therefore, there is no universally accepted definition of this complex phenomenon.

13

Summary

The present day experiences of black young people as they move from school to work cannot be viewed in isolation. Afro-Caribbean and Asian young people have a history linked directly with Britain's imperial past and concepts of 'race' developed then still influence how black people are seen today. Their parents or grandparents were mostly part of an immigration process to Britain and experienced direct discrimination in housing and employment when they arrived. The education system was slow to respond to the needs of immigrants and to the different needs of their children and grandchildren, living in a multicultural society. The policy response to widespread employment discrimination was also slow. It is this that forms the backdrop to a study of the experiences of ethnic minority young people in the mid eighties. What now needs to be considered is the empirical evidence about the factors affecting young people in their move into the labour market during the period of the late 1980s.

2 The issues reviewed

Introduction

The purpose of this chapter is to review previous studies about the educational experiences of ethnic minority young people aged 16-19 and also to review previous studies about their labour market experiences. In education these topics include attainment in examinations at 16, the decision about whether or not to stay on in post-compulsory education, how people attempt to improve on their qualifications, the academic and vocational qualifications young people seek to obtain and how they progress into higher education.

On the labour market I will examine the evidence for ethnic differences in YTS, in employment and in unemployment. The factors advanced to explain these differences will then be considered and the weight given to these different factors in various studies examined. There is surprisingly little recent data on some of these topics, particularly on post-compulsory education. More attention has been focused on attainment at 16, partly as a result of the Swann Report (DES 1985) and it is of particular interest to review the quality of the data and the conclusions of this set of studies.

Examination results at 16

More than a decade has passed since the government set up a Committee of Inquiry into the Education of Children from Ethnic Minority Groups. In their final report Lord Swann's Committee concluded that 'West Indian children as a group are under achieving in our education system and this should be a matter of deep concern not

15

only to all those involved in education but also the whole community' (DES, 1985). Despite the considerable volume of debate, however, the Swann Committee became acutely aware of the lack of statistical data available to them to test their hypotheses. The report commented, in particular, on the inadequacy of official statistics to provide anything but the crudest indications of the extent of differences between ethnic groups in academic achievement as well as on the limited and small-scale nature of the research in universities, colleges and research institutes.

Matters have improved a little since then. In the eighties a variety of studies were published and in this chapter the major British studies that have appeared are reviewed. What light do they throw on the relative importance of social background, community and related factors? To what extent do they address the question of whether schools affect children's performance to any major degree? And to what extent have their results depended on the underlying conceptual frameworks they have embodied and the statistical procedures they have employed?

In selecting studies for review I deliberately confined myself to those which contained data about the examination performances of ethnic minority and white pupils at the end of their period of compulsory schooling (i.e. 16-plus). I was able to identify nine studies in all which are listed in Table 2.1. This shows: the year to which the study's exam results related (this was often quite a lot earlier than the date of publication); the size of the samples obtained, with particular reference to the numbers of cases describing Afro-Caribbean and Asian pupils; the nature and location of the samples of schools and local authorities on which the survey was based; and the nature of the data on social background and/or prior attainment that were collected.

I should, perhaps, stress that these do not constitute the total of relevant studies about the influences on the achievements of young people from ethnic minority backgrounds but they do provide a common focus for comparison and concern. The attention of readers who wish to obtain some overview of the whole field is drawn to the comprehensive accounts by, for example, Tomlinson (1983), Taylor (1981), Taylor and Hegarty (1985) and Gillborn (1990). A previous review of some of the statistical aspects of research on these questions has been provided by Plewis (1988). To the best of my knowledge, however, no one has attempted a comprehensive critique of the research conducted since Swann from a primarily statistical point of view.

A matter of research design

Looking at the nine studies that have been published over the past decade it rapidly becomes clear that each possesses different strengths and weaknesses from the point of view of research design. The three dominant approaches' researchers have employed are outlined in Figure 2.1.

Most of the studies have embodied a cross-sectional dimension. If data are gathered on young people's performance at the age of 16 plus what can be said about the factors which are associated with (perhaps even caused) differences in performance between ethnic minority and white groups? Typically, such research designs collect information on aspects of social background, gender and, occasionally, neighbourhood or social context at one particular point in time. Evidence about the potential effects of attending different schools has only infrequently been collected and has not featured very prominently in any subsequent analyses.

A second kind of study has incorporated a longitudinal component. Data on pupils' test performances at 11 plus may have been assembled or collected in tandem with data on 16 plus exam results. Such research designs permit conclusions to be drawn about the progress pupils have made between the two time points. Of course, the progress pupils make during the period of their compulsory schooling and the qualifications they finally obtain are not the same thing. Progress is measured relative to the pupils' starting points. A major focus of such studies has been to explore the extent to which such progress has been associated with ethnic background and related factors, as well as whether the position of particular sub groups has collectively improved or declined relative to the norm. Again evidence about the effects of attending different schools has scarcely figured.

Seven of the nine studies I considered have been largely confined to one or other of these first two research designs. Only two of those I review here have been built upon research designs which have deliberately incorporated 'the school attended' as a factor in the research strategy. Such multi level approaches have only recently begun to emerge and much remains to be understood about them, both in terms of their strengths and their potential limitations.

The multi level studies attempt to answer two questions simultaneously. First, they try to establish the extent to which the

Table 2.1: Features of the British studies comparing examination performance at 16 for ethnic minority groups

Study and author (s)	Year of exam results	Sample size total/ Afro-Caribbean/ Asian	Nature of sample	Control for social background and intake
Maughan & Rutter (1986)	1972	2,286 250 Not stated	12 non-selective secondary schools in 6 Inner London boroughs	Gender. Seven point teacher-ratings of verbal reasoning ability at 11. Reading test scores at 14.
Driver (1980)	1974-77	2,310 590 508	5 mixed comprehensives in 5 LEAs in North, Midlands and Home Counties	Gender
Mabey (1986)	1976	21,662 2,382 389	All pupils in a single cohort of ILEA schools	Gender. Reading attainment at 15. Assessed verbal reasoning ability at secondary school transfer.
Craft & Craft (1983)	1979	2,237 207 524	16 schools in one Outer London borough	Gender and social class
Eggleston et al (1986)	1981	562 110 157	23 comprehensives in 6 LEAs	Gender
DES (1985)	1979 1982	6,196 718 466 5,942 653 571	A 10% sample of pupils in 6/5 LEAs with high numbers ethnic minority pupils	None

Keysel (1988)	1985	17,058 2,981 1,124	All pupils in a single cohort of ILEA schools	Gender. Verbal reasoning band at 11. (3 groups)
Smith & Tomlinson (1989)	1986	1,154 146 664	18 schools in 4 LEAs	Gender, socio-economic group and second year reading score
Nuttall, Goldstein *et al* (1989)	1985-87	31,623 Not stated	Pupils in 3 cohorts of ILEA schools	Gender, verbal reasoning band, school type and proportion with free school meals.

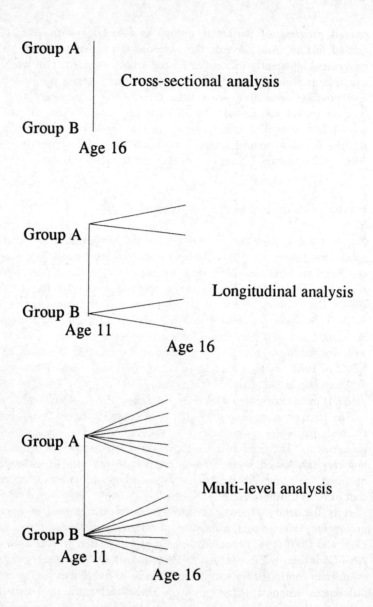

Figure 2.1 Three different research designs

overall progress of particular groups is associated with ethnically related factors. And second, they explore the extent to which such progress is apparently influenced by the school attended. Can we, for example, confidently assert that if ethnic minority young people make less progress over five years than their white equivalents this is because (either substantially or in part) they attend 'less effective' schools? A school's 'effectiveness' in this context is, of course, relative to what other schools achieved with pupils whose starting points were similar at the point of entry to secondary school.

Estimates of the gap in exam achievement

Our first task is to obtain an overview of the size of the gap in exam achievement between different ethnic minority groups and their white counterparts. I have already listed the major design features of all the studies in Table 2.1. They present a relatively stable picture of the association between ethnic origin and educational achievement (see Table 2.2). As a group it would appear that Afro-Caribbean pupils performed less well than others in terms of the proportions of students who reached the highest levels of exam achievement. In the study of 6 LEAs in 1981, for example, 15 per cent of all pupils and 18 per cent of Asian pupils had achieved five or more 'higher grade' (A-C or CSE grade 1) passes compared with only 7 per cent of Afro-Caribbeans.

The 'five or more passes' hurdle is, of course, a rather 'high' one, reached by only a minority of pupils, whatever their ethnic backgrounds. The same analysis shows that such differences persisted, however, at 'lower' levels as well. About 46 per cent of all pupils obtained one or more higher grade passes compared with only 35 per cent of Afro-Caribbeans.

It is frequently argued that differences in attainments of ethnic groups are, in large part, a function of differences in social class. But Craft and Craft (1983) concluded that the examination performance of Afro-Caribbean pupils 'lagged behind that of all the other groups, even when controlled for social class'. Some of the studies find gender differences amongst ethnic groups. These differences are usually rather smaller than those associated with other factors but, as a general rule, girls have tended to do better than boys (Driver 1980; Mac an Ghaill, 1988; Mirza, 1992).

21

Table 2.2: Exam results broken down by ethnic origin: a comparison of the results from six surveys

Study, Location and Year of Exam Results (a)	No. Exams Taken (%)	No. Graded Passes (%)	1+ CSE 4/5 (%)	1+ CSE 2/3 (%)	1-4 'O' Levels (%)	5+ 'O' Levels (%)	Total (%)	No. of Cases
Afro-Caribbean								
1) London, 1972 (b)	(——17——)		18	44	20	0	100	250
2) Inner London, 1976	11	7	29	40	21	2	100	2,382
3) 6 LEAs, 1979	(——17——)		(——80——)			3	100	718
4) 6 LEAs, 1981	(——8——)		(——57——)		28	7	100	110
5) 5 LEAs, 1982	(——19——)		(——75——)			6	100	653
6) Inner London, 1985	14	3	13	38	27	5	100	2,981
Asian								
1) London, 1972 (b)			not available					389
2) Inner London, 1976	14	3	8	29	27	17	100	389
3) 6 LEAs, 1979	(——20——)		(——63——)			17	100	466
4) 6 LEAs, 1981	(——6——)		(——48——)		29	18	101	157
5) 5 LEAs, 1982	(——19——)		(——64——)			17	100	571
6) Inner London, 1985	16	2	8	26	30	18	100	1,124

Total Sample (all pupils) (c)

	A	B	C	D	E	F		
1) London, 1972(b)	(------30------)		12	31	23	3	100	2,018
2) Inner London, 1976	19	8	11	27	26	10	100	24,398
3) 6 LEAs, 1979	(------21------)	(------64------)			15	100	6,196
4) 6 LEAs, 1981	(------9------)	(------45------)		31	15	100	548
5) 5 LEAs, 1982	(------19------)	(------63------)			18	100	5,942
6) Inner London, 1985	19	3	9	29	30	10	100	17,058

Notes:

(a) The year referred to here is that in which the exams were taken. Publications sometimes followed several years later.

(b) Fuller details of the studies may be found in the references as follows: (1) Maughan and Rutter (1986); (2) Mabey (1986); (3)and (5) Department of Education & Science (1985), one LEA dropped out of the later survey; (4) Eggleston (1986); (6) Kysel (1988)

(c) Includes Afro-Caribbean, Asian, white and other ethnic groups.

23

Sampling strategies

It is well understood amongst statisticians that sample designs affect the estimates made of population characteristics. Researchers looking at ethnic minority groups have been well aware of these problems. In particular, in any such study, two questions emerge.

The first is whether to concentrate the study in a limited number of geographical areas. The main areas of ethnic concentration are also the ones characterized by high levels of social deprivation. The researcher is balancing the requirement for some kind of representativeness against the need to obtain sizeable numbers of ethnic minority pupils who, by their very minority status, are not likely to be available in large numbers wherever the research is located.

The second question is how to draw a sample of schools within the areas chosen? Schools with higher concentrations of ethnic minority pupils may not be generally representative of all the schools in a particular area, let alone nationally. For a mixture of theoretical and pragmatic reasons the various studies have adopted different strategies, the practical consequences of which were listed in Table 2.1 earlier. By far the most popular location for research has been the London conurbation and four of the studies concentrated exclusively on this area. None of the studies listed was a nationally representative one. The highest number of LEAs used in any of the studies was six and these were specifically selected to have high percentages of ethnic minority children and to be situated in inner city areas. Whilst the sheer size of London makes it of interest, few would argue that it is necessarily representative of the country as a whole.

Within particular areas the choice of individual schools is also important. It has been argued that, by choosing fairly equal numbers of ethnic minority and white pupils from the same schools in the same areas, then one can ensure that ethnic minority children do not attend less effective schools or live in more socially disadvantaged areas than white ones. But this is only a very approximate solution to the problem. It may also remove, of course, the probability of explaining one of the reasons why such performances may differ, namely differences in the effectiveness of the schools attended.

In brief, researchers are now more aware of the need to generate more nationally representative samples of areas and schools to answer some of the questions which are of central interest to this particular debate.

24

Focusing on progress

Three studies (those by Maughan and Rutter, Mabey and Kysel) have looked at the progress young people have made during the course of their secondary school years. All three have capitalised on the existence in the Inner London Education Authority of measures of pupils' attainment at the age of 11, the point of transfer to secondary school.

The focus on pupils' 'progress' coincided with renewed interest in studies of school effectiveness during the early eighties but it should not be confused with it. In fact, none of them focused specifically on the schools' contribution at all.

Maughan and Rutter (1986) attempted to explore whether ethnic background was associated with pupils' progress over both a two and five year period. In one analysis predicting exam results at 16 plus, they controlled for reading test scores at 14, gender and ethnic origin; in another they used Verbal Reasoning scores (based on a seven point scale) at 11 plus. In both cases they found that ethnic differences were not statistically significant. Commenting on their findings they reported that they 'gave no evidence of any relative deterioration or improvement in the performance of ethnic minority (West Indian) candidates over this period; their results at 16 plus, although poorer in absolute terms than those of whites, were essentially as might have been expected on the basis of their earlier attainment'. Ethnic background, in other words, did not appear to affect progress; whatever the differences between ethnic groups that had emerged by the age of eleven they were not much altered over the following five years.

Both the other studies using data from the ILEA reported that ethnic minority pupils were making the same or greater progress, relatively speaking, as other groups. Mabey (1986) controlled for reading test scores at 15, ethnic origin and gender in her analysis. Adjusting for reading scores at 15 gave the average Afro-Caribbean pupil a score one and a half points higher than that of his or her white counterparts. In other words, given their prior reading attainment, they were achieving more than would have been predicted. Some doubts about this particular finding must be retained, however, since reading at 15 is rather close in time to exam performance at 16 plus. If, for any reason, the Afro-Caribbean scores were 'depressed' at 15 then this could well have shown up as 'greater progress' at 16 plus.

Kysel (1988) used the pupils' Verbal Reasoning (VR) scores at the point of transfer to secondary school along with gender and ethnic origin. She first predicted exam results at 16 using sex and VR band alone, then looked at the additional contribution of ethnic origin. She found it to be statistically significant. There were also statistically significant interactions between VR band and ethnic groups and between VR band and gender. The results actually achieved by white pupils were worse than those predicted using VR band and gender alone, suggesting that it was the white pupils who were making the least progress. However, Kysel herself expressed some doubts about this conclusion.

The control for prior attainment she adopted was a relatively crude one with VR Band divided into just three groups with pupils allocated to one of three bands: the top 25 per cent, the next 50 per cent and the bottom 25 per cent. In addition the allocation of pupils to the three groups was based on teacher based assessments rather than actual test results obtained. Previous work on teachers' expectations of Afro-Caribbean pupils suggests that it is possible that, in these cases, more ethnic minority pupils might have been inappropriately allocated by their teachers to the lower bands than their white counterparts. The apparent progress they subsequently made might then merely have reflected these earlier inappropriate assignments.

There are, of course, other interpretations. Afro-Caribbean pupils could, for example, receive increased levels of parental support during their secondary years or increase their own levels of motivation by other means. In both cases, these increases would have to be over and above any increases experienced by white and other groups. Alternatively, their greater progress could result from their attending more effective schools; again, this would be relative to other ethnic groups. Whilst the literature does not rule these possibilities out, it does not provide direct support for them either.

In brief, I believe the most plausible explanation for the greater 'progress' of the Afro-Caribbean pupils is that teachers' assessments at the age of eleven were relatively inaccurate, especially when contrasted with the procedures of public examinations at 16 plus.

Strictly speaking, the conclusions of these various studies of progress ought to be confined to the areas and schools covered by the LEA. But, whatever the case, the available evidence does not support the widely held view that pupils from ethnic minority backgrounds in general (and from Afro-Caribbean ones in particular) made less progress during their secondary school years than their white counterparts. Whether this conclusion really stands up is a matter to which I direct closer attention in the next section where I consider in greater detail the studies that have something to say more directly about schools' effectiveness.

Studies of school effectiveness

There have been a number of studies of school effectiveness over the past decade. Only two, however, are particularly germane to the present debate insofar as they contain an ethnic dimension.

Both studies are sufficiently recent for them to have been able to take advantage of the latest statistical procedures known as multi level modelling (see Goldstein, 1987, for a fuller account and Gray, Jesson and Sime, 1990, for an example). The advantages of this approach over previous research are two fold. First, the effects of schools are explicitly modelled in the analysis. And second, it is possible to test whether schools are differentially effective for particular subgroups, such as ethnic minorities. Do ethnic minority pupils, in other words, make greater progress in some kinds of schools as opposed to others?

The multi level model can, for convenience, be described as containing two stages. In the first stage a regression analysis is conducted to establish the overall average relationship between the predictor variables (which, on this occasion, include measures of pupils' prior attainment) and the outcomes (pupils' exam results). This is known as the fixed part of the model and it is assumed to be the same for children in every school. In the second stage (know as the random part of the model) a separate regression analysis is conducted for the pupils within each school. This allows one to see how far schools differ in terms of the average differences between them (the school effects). It also allows the nature of the relationship between the predictor variables and the outcomes within schools to be established. Some schools may be widening the gap between the most able and least able pupils, for example, relative to other schools (see Figure 2.2). It is also possible to establish whether, having controlled for all other variables, ethnic minority pupils progress more (relative to white pupils) in some schools as opposed to others.

In the first of the two studies to be published Smith and Tomlinson (1989) reported that Asian and West Indian pupils made significantly better progress than white pupils, when allowance was made for both social class and their attainment in reading at the end of the second year of secondary schooling. At the same time they found that the differences in schools' average effectiveness were quite large. A pupil who attended a school which just fell into the top quarter of

27

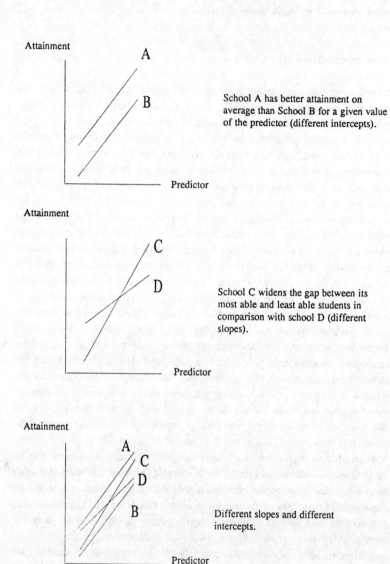

Figure 2.2 Two kinds of school effects

28

effectiveness obtained, on average, about two more 'high grade' O level passes (or their equivalent) than one who attended a school which just fell into the bottom quarter of effectiveness.

Furthermore, following up the theme of differential effectiveness, they reported that ethnic minority pupils made greater progress in some schools than others, although the actual extent of these differences was not made clear; it was certainly a good deal smaller than the average school effects. Overall, they concluded that 'some schools (were) much better than others and the ones that (were) good for white pupils tended to be about equally good for ethnic minority pupils' as well. (Smith and Tomlinson 1989: 305). The main drawback of the Smith and Tomlinson research design is the strategy they adopted for sampling schools. Their sample was a 'purposive' selection of 18 schools within four LEAs, deliberately chosen to offer a wide range of characteristics and qualities. Eventually, given the very real practical constraints on the sample size, it was impossible to obtain a full mix of schools with both large and small numbers (and proportions) of Afro-Caribbean and Asian pupils, reflecting the full range of social class differences as well. Most of the Bangladeshi pupils, for example, were concentrated in a single girls' school. The number of Afro-Caribbean pupils was also small at the end of the study (only 146 at 16-plus) and, as a consequence, they were combined with the group defined as 'mixed or other' for some analyses, a far from ideal situation. The authors were consequently rather tentative about the differential effectiveness of the various schools as far as ethnic minority pupils were concerned, although some further analyses I have conducted based on the published data suggest that more of them probably went to the less effective schools (table not shown).

Nuttall and Goldstein's (1989) analysis of pupil data on over 30,000 pupils in some 140 ILEA secondary schools is certainly the largest of the studies of schools to date. They concluded that, in general, the progress of pupils from ethnic minority backgrounds was as good (if not better) as that of white young people. There was an exception to this general trend; Afro-Caribbeans made slightly less (not significantly worse) progress. They too reported differences in the average effects of different schools as well as some evidence of differential effectiveness. Amongst Afro-Caribbean pupils of the (apparently) same prior attainments, schools could differ in the predicted attainment for this group by as much as one 'high grade' O level pass when the full range of school differences was considered; amongst Pakistani pupils the differences could amount to as much as two O level passes. Nuttall and Goldstein concluded, as a result, that it did not make sense to talk of schools which were universally effective or ineffective; there was no single dimension of school effectiveness.

The large sample size of the Nuttall and Goldstein study is an obvious strength as is the existence of prior attainment measures in the form of Verbal Reasoning Band scores. As we noted in relation to some of the previous ILEA studies, however, the rather crude (three category) nature of this variable makes it less adequate than might at first appear. Also, as with the Kysel study which we discussed earlier, the possibility of teachers making inappropriate assignments of pupils from ethnic minority backgrounds to the three VR Bands cannot be ruled out. It would also have been useful to have had some information on pupils' social class backgrounds as these might have contributed to explaining the differences in exam attainment, over and above the part explained by the relatively crude measure of prior attainment used in this study.

My interest in these studies of school effectiveness was initially aroused because I felt they might contribute to my understanding of the factors creating the ethnic minority-white achievement gap. Could a major reason why the ethnic minority pupils performed less well be because they attended less effective schools?

The two studies help to unravel some parts of this conundrum but not, unfortunately, others. My first task was to establish what they said about average school effects. In other words, are some schools in the areas where the majority of ethnic minority pupils receive their education, markedly more effective than others? The answer provided by both those surveys reviewed here is a positive one. Pupils in some of the schools in both studies were, on average obtaining considerably better results than 'similar' pupils in other schools in the same area. The size of the differences is less easily determined, however, and needs to be viewed in the context of other estimates (see, for example, Gray, Jesson and Sime 1990). Suffice it to say that the average differences in school effects reported could be sufficiently large to account for the reported differences in the average exam performances of ethnic minority and white pupils.

Our second question is whether the schools in the two studies were differentially effective for different sub-groups (and especially ethnic minority pupils). Both provide some evidence for this, although that provided in the Nuttall and Goldstein study is considerably stronger than in the Smith and Tomlinson one. And, again the reported size of these effects is sufficiently large to go some way towards explaining the exam achievement gap.

On both the question of school effects and the question of differential effectiveness, therefore, the studies provide support for the view that schools make some difference. To what extent, then, do pupils from ethnic minority backgrounds (and especially Afro-Caribbeans) attend less effective schools than their white counterparts?

Unfortunately, but frustratingly, both studies have rather little to say on this topic. In the case of the Smith and Tomlinson research there are probably two reasons for this. One reason is that the researchers' conclusions were inevitably confined to those schools that had originally been selected as part of their sampling strategy. How effective overall their 18 schools were compared to others cannot be established. Another reason may be that they were clearly more impressed by the average differences between schools than by anything else about them. Which particular school a pupil went to clearly mattered. The question of whether pupils from particular ethnic groups were attending more or less effective schools, in greater or lesser numbers, was a subsidiary question and one that was not given attention. I have also discussed other limitations of Smith and Tomlinson's study and controversies arising from it, in particular the way the study was unable to deal with racism in the lived experience of ethnic minority pupils and made potentially misleading conclusions in this respect (see Gillborn and Drew, 1992; Gillborn and Drew, 1993).

Nuttall and Goldstein's study provide better estimates of the extent of average differences between schools than Smith and Tomlinson's. Their reason for not pursuing the particular question I have posed seems to have been based on their interpretation of the studies as showing that schools could not be ranked in terms of a single dimension of effectiveness. In the context of current debates about the evaluation of schools' performance this is a useful point to make. It would nevertheless, have been possible (if a little time consuming) to characterise the patterns of effectiveness of individual ILEA schools and to then explore whether these were related in any systematic way to the experiences of ethnic minority groups. This particular extension of their analyses remains a priority for the issues reviewed here.

In brief, neither of these two studies relating to schools' effectiveness provide convincing evidence about the schools' contribution to the existence of the ethnic minority-white gap in achievement.

The agenda for this review was set by the Swann Committee some years ago. Progress since then has been slow. Parekh (1983) has commented on the 'fallacy of the single factor', the view that somehow the family or Afro-Caribbean culture or whatever was the factor of overriding importance in explaining the achievement gap. The earlier studies considered here have been stronger on the social background side but their limitations have been clear. By ignoring possible influences at the level of the school they have had a tendency to 'blame the victim'. The later studies have been somewhat stronger on the school's potential role and provide a useful correction of emphasis. Schools certainly differ to some considerable extent in their effectiveness, but whether they are *the* major contributing factor remains unclear. To date we lack a study with a sufficient number of pupils and schools, covering a sufficient range of variables, with a nationally representative sample, combining both qualitative and quantitative forms of data gathering to answer the questions Swann posed. Writing in 1984 Troyna warned that the 'greatest danger lies in the possibility that ill-conceived and poorly formulated studies will perpetuate the notion of ethnic minority educational under achievement as a given rather than as a problematic that requires sensitive and systematic interrogation' (Troyna 1984: 164). The dangers today are still as great as they were then.

Post-compulsory education

In this section a summary is given of the relevant studies that have been recently published with their limitations in terms of sample size. Then the major issues recurring in these surveys are discussed.

There is surprisingly little data on post-compulsory education. Maughan and Rutter (1986) followed a sample of pupils attending 12 ILEA multi-ethnic comprehensive schools through the sixth forms and focused on Afro-Caribbean pupils, of whom there were some 250. These young people were entering post-compulsory education in 1972 so this information is now rather dated. So too are the data used by Craft and Craft (1983) who studied students in a single LEA in Greater London in 1979. Some data on A level results is available from the DES School Leavers Survey (DES, 1985) but again this is very limited. Eggleston and his colleagues (1986) followed a group of ethnic minority and white young people from 23 comprehensive schools through secondary education and into sixth form or further education colleges but only as far as the first post-compulsory year;

this study too is constrained by an overall sample size of just over 800. The strengths and weaknesses of these various studies are discussed in more detail elsewhere (Drew and Gray, 1991).

Cross, Wrench and Barnett (1990) carried out a survey on ethnic minorities and the Careers Service. This study is recent and contains useful data on both participation in education and the context in which career decisions are made. Their sample contained over 300 Afro-Caribbean and 700 Asian respondents. They collected some qualitative data but, in general, few ethnographic studies have been carried out with students after the end of compulsory schooling, the ones by Mac an Ghaill (1988, 1989) being rare examples.

A study of 608 people was conducted for the Voice newspaper by Scott (1990) to investigate the school experiences and career aspirations of Afro-Caribbean 16-30 year olds. The sample consisted of people replying to an advertisement in the Voice or completing a questionnaire in the newspaper and was therefore not a random or statistically representative one in any sense. The potential is there for the results to be seriously biased.

Connolly, Roberts, Ben Tovim and Torkington (1992) interviewed 134 ethnic minority young people in Liverpool in 1989 and used their data to make comparisons with data collected for the ESRC 16-19 Initiative. Again the sample size is rather small.

Jones (1993) used data from the Labour Force Survey aggregated over the period 1988-90 to focus on education, employment and housing.

A number of issues recur in these studies. The first major issue is the decision to stay on in post-compulsory education and the factors that affect this decision. There is a complex set of factors. They include attitudes about the education system and expectations of finding employment in a labour market in recession. They also include the advice given by parents, peers, the school and careers advisers (Micklewright, Pearson and Smith, 1990).

Whilst these factors affect all young people, ethnic minority young people are faced with particular pressures and conflicting advice. A number of studies have shown that ethnic minorities have a strong motivation towards self improvement through educational achievement. It is also the case that ethnic minority young people will find it more difficult to obtain employment than their white peers (Clough, Drew and Jones, 1988). The combination of recession and labour market racism mean that prospects for employment are relatively poor. Staying on could, in part, be a means to defer entry into a difficult labour market (Eggleston et al 1986: 240). Connolly et

33

al (1992) report a mixed set of attitudes to qualifications from their ethnic minority respondents. Some were negative. 'My school qualifications are foolish ... not worth anything ... haven't helped at all'. Others were positive. 'Most employers ask for them ... Without qualifications you're at a disadvantage straight away'. The respondents in Connolly's study were Afro-Caribbean and living mainly in Liverpool and therefore their pessimism may have been well founded as youth unemployment rates were very high there.

The high academic and occupational aspirations of ethnic minority young people are highlighted by Cross, Wrench and Barnett (1990) in their study of careers advisers. Such enthusiasm was not universally encouraged though. This study focused on the issue of 'over aspiration' of ethnic minority young people as perceived by careers advisers. Asian young people tended to achieve more highly than other groups in the school, yet their desire to stay on in education tended to be judged negatively in terms of an ignorance of the realities of the labour market and unwarranted and misguided parental pressure. The belief amongst careers staff that ethnic minority young people would do better to leave full-time education appeared to come through regardless of academic performance. This tendency for teachers and other professionals to describe Asian pupils as 'over aspiring' is also taken up by other authors (Brah and Golding, 1983).

The career aspirations of 376 fifth formers in three Rochdale comprehensive schools were studied by Penn and Scattergood (1992). The study concluded that there was little evidence of any important school effect and that aspirations for higher education are determined both by a marked ethnic effect and a strong social class effect amongst non-Asians. Whilst the Automatic Interaction Detection method utilised here is a little used and potentially powerful one for exploring interactions (I used it myself in a nationally representative study of schools in the late sixties, see Drew, 1972) any conclusions, particularly those about school effects, are severely limited by the size and scope of the sample in the survey by Penn and Scattergood.

The second major issue is the high participation rate of ethnic minority young people in post-compulsory education. Craft and Craft (1983) found that the whilst only 44 per cent of white young people stayed on, over 50 per cent of West Indians did so and over 80 per cent of Asians. These rates varied by attainment at 16. Cross, Wrench and Barnett (1990) found high ethnic minority participation rates except for Afro-Caribbean males, as did Jones (1993).

A third major issue is the way in which ethnic minority young people use the post-compulsory education period. Some researchers have noted that the staying on period is utilised in different ways; to take or retake academic courses or to move on to vocational courses (Connolly et al 1992). There has been little study of the pattern of participation in this respect, mainly because there have been few recent studies which have included further education colleges (Eggleston et al, 1986). Some authors have suggested a tendency for Asians to pursue academic qualifications and for Afro-Caribbeans to study for vocational qualifications and Cross et al (1990) have noted the danger that this has become a stereotype amongst careers advisers. The relationship between the choices made at the post 16 stage and attainment at 16 has not been adequately explored.

A final major issue is the outcomes of the post-compulsory period, the results of this period of study and the transitions that take place at this point into the higher education sector. Craft and Craft (1983) reported lower levels of A level performance for the ethnic minority groups relative to the white group and smaller numbers entering higher education. But this data is very dated and only for one area in London. More recent data on admissions to university (Taylor, 1992) suggest that the numbers of ethnic minority applicants are increasing but such applicants tend to have lower A level scores than white applicants. Students from ethnic minority groups were concentrated in particular areas: social sciences, medicine and dentistry for example. These were often high demand courses requiring high A level scores and therefore chances of success were limited.

The youth labour market

In this section a summary is given of the relevant studies that have recently been published with their limitations in terms of sample size. After this the literature is examined in more detail by considering the factors that have been included in studies on the employment and unemployment chances of young people. The object of this is to reflect on the emphases that different authors have placed on these factors, coming as they do from rather different positions and with the limitations of the data they had available to them. This leads on in the later chapters to the way I have attempted to take account of the important factors in the analysis of my data.

The number of recent studies on the labour market experiences of ethnic minority young people is relatively small. Some details of selected studies are given in Table 2.3 providing information on the

Table 2.3: Features of selected British studies of ethnic differences in the youth labour market

Study and author (s)	Year data collected	Sample sizes total/Afro-Caribbean/ Asian	Nature of sample
Daniel (1968) 1st PEP/PSI	1966	974 540 333	6 areas of Britain. The 2 wards in each area with the highest density of immigrant population were selected
Dept. of Employment Labour Force Survey	1984-	60,000 overall sample each year in Gt Britain since 1984	Multi-stage stratified random survey.
Smith (1974) 2nd PEP/PSI Study	1974	A sample of 283 employers	A survey of 283 employers at plant level. Excluded areas with small immigrant population. 3 separate regions: North, Midlands, South
Wrench and Lee (1983)	1979	697 169 226	Fifth form pupils in four Birmingham Schools
Smith (1981)	1979	2,454 524 946	A survey of the unemployed, 18 employment areas sampled.
Roberts, Noble and Duggan (1983)	1979	551 250 -	Six multi-racial neighbourhoods; Brixton, Harlesden, Shepherds Bush, Toxteth, Moss Side, Wolverhampton.
Banks, Ullah and Warr (1984)	1982	1,150 374 -	Quota sample of youth unemployed aged 17 in 11 geographical areas
Brown (1984) 3rd PEP/PSI Study	1982	7,306 1,650 3,350	2 samples, one of white respondents, the other of ethnic minority respondents. 2,560 clusters of 1000 EDs selected.
Clough, Drew and Jones (1985)	1983	2,818 93 264	Young people aged 16-18 sampled from Careers Service records in Sheffield and Bradford.

Cross, Wrench and Barnett (1990)	1985	896 166 282	Matched sample selected from Careers Service records in nine areas.
Jones (1993)	1988-90	54,203* 762 1,774	Labour Force Survey
Connolly et al (1992)	1989	1,228 126 15	1,094 in general sample of Liverpool 17-19 year olds plus special sample 134 blacks.

Note:
* Numbers in 16-24 age group in survey.

year data was collected, the overall sample size, the number of Afro-Caribbean and Asian respondents and the nature of the sample.

A particularly useful study is that by Cross, Wrench and Barnett (1990). This builds on the detailed survey by Sillitoe and Meltzer (1985) which, although recently published, used data collected in the early seventies. A regular series of articles analysing ethnic differences in the Labour Force Survey is published by the Department of Employment (see, for example, Department of Employment, 1990) although the analysis is mainly limited to labour market activities broken down by ethnic origin. This led to a more comprehensive analysis of this data using information aggregated over a three year period 1988-90 (Jones 1993).

Looking back at research published during the last decade the studies have usually been either small or based on local labour markets. The data in the Policy Studies Institute study (Brown 1984) are an exception to this, being a nationally representative sample; however, the data were collected in the early part of the eighties and are now becoming dated. Researchers at PSI and its precursor, Political and Economic Planning, (PEP) have been responsible for studies over more than two decades and provide important continuity in research in this area (Daniel, 1968; Smith, 1974; Smith, 1981; Brown, 1984 and Jones 1993).

The labour market at 16 was also covered in a study by Eggleston and his colleagues (1986) but the sample size at this stage was small (125 respondents). The survey carried out for the Commission for Racial Equality on ethnic minority school leavers looking for work in Lewisham in 1977 (CRE 1978) was repeated in 1988 but again this was small-scale. A number of earlier studies are cited in Troyna and Smith (1983) (for example, the survey by Wrench and Lee) and studies of young people's experiences within YTS in Cross and Smith (1987). Other surveys are reported by Brah and Golding (1983), Banks, Ullah and Warr (1984), Verma and Darby (1987) writing about West Yorkshire and Connolly, Roberts, Ben-Tovim and Torkington (1992) writing about 134 ethnic minority young people in Liverpool.

Few studies have examined ethnic differences using models. Clough and Drew (1985) have used logit analysis to model unemployment rates in Sheffield and Bradford and Whitfield and Bourlakis (1989) have used probit analysis to model employment probabilities after YTS.

There are various possible factors which affect an individual's chances of being in employment. Some of these factors are economic

38

and structural and others operate at the level of the individual. Some affect ethnic minority young people differently to white young people. What I shall now do is briefly discuss the evidence for inequalities and then discuss the main factors in turn that have been advanced to explain these differences.

There are marked differences in unemployment rates. Ethnic minority unemployment rates have generally been higher than those of the population taken as a whole over all age groups. Data taken from the Labour Force Survey illustrate this (Figure 2.3). At a time of increasing unemployment ethnic minority unemployment rises particularly rapidly. For ethnic minority young people the Labour Force Survey suggests that the Pakistani and Bangladeshi group is worst affected with the unemployment rate for this group and the Afro-Caribbean group more than double that of whites (Figure 2.4). The differences between white and ethnic minority unemployment rates also persist by region (Figure 2.5) and within cities (Figure 2.6).

What are the reasons for these differences? Level of educational attainment is clearly an important factor although a number of surveys have shown that qualifications alone only partly explain the ethnic differences in unemployment rates in general (Jones 1993) and youth unemployment rates in particular (Roberts, Noble and Duggan, 1983; Clough, Drew and Jones 1988). In the latter survey, for those with 'high' qualifications in Sheffield the unemployment rate for ethnic minority young people was approximately three times that for similar white young people.

These surveys however only made use of fairly crude attainment differences at the O level stage. A more detailed analysis would focus on the way individuals build on their qualifications at the post 16 stage, either with academic or with vocational qualifications and how this affects their employment chances. It is useful to think of the choices made between 16 and 19 in terms of 'routes' into the youth labour market (Sime, Pattie and Gray, 1990); whether to stay on and study for academic or vocational qualifications, whether to leave school at 16 and seek work immediately, whether to take up a YTS place and so on. There may be ethnic differences in a number of these respects.

There is evidence of ethnic differences in YTS participation. Two studies sponsored by the Manpower Services Commission (Cross et al, 1983 and Fenton et al 1984) pointed to several areas of concern. Fenton's study of YTS showed that ethnic minority young people were concentrated in mode B (college based) schemes. Although mode A (employer based) schemes were not necessarily superior in the

39

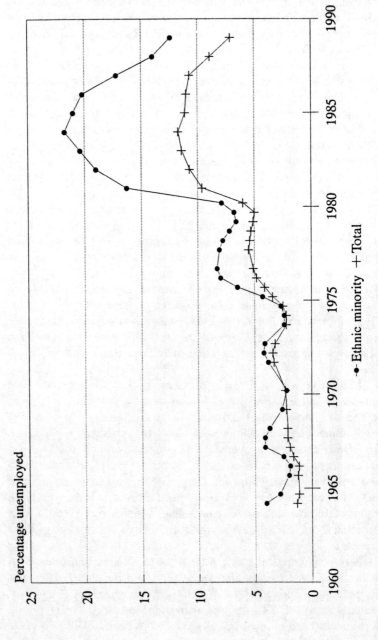

Figure 2.3 Total and ethnic minority unemployment rates 1963-1989

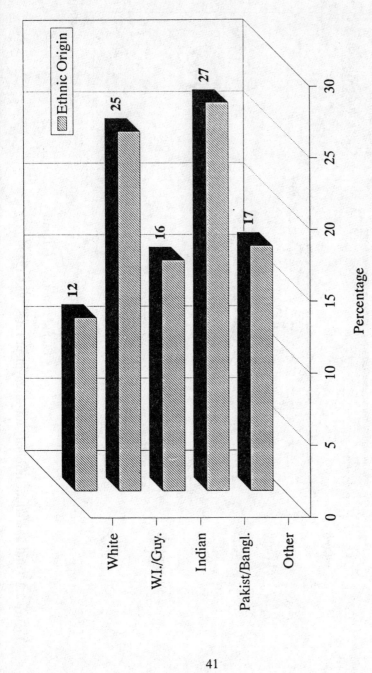

Figure 2.4 Youth unemployment rates by ethnic origin 1987-1989

41

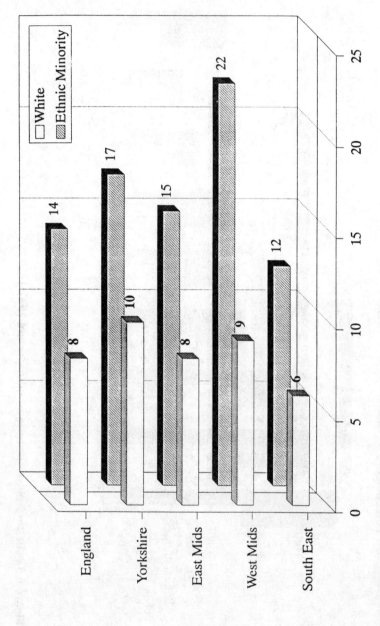

Figure 2.5 Unemployment rates by ethnic origin and region 1987-1989

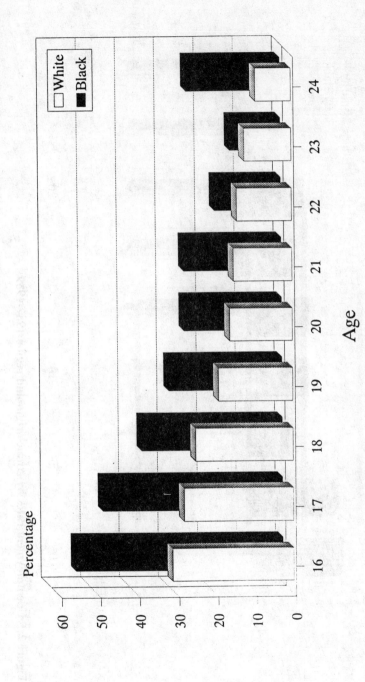

Figure 2.6 Female unemployment rates by ethnic origin and age, Sheffield 1981

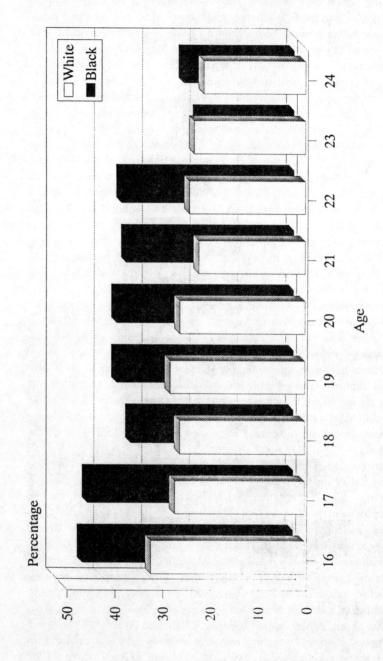

Figure 2.7 Male unemployment rates by ethnic origin and age, Sheffield 1981

44

training which they provided, they were regarded by some as more prestigious than mode B schemes and there is clear evidence that mode A trainees had a much better chance of subsequent employment. For this reason the issue of allocation of ethnic minority young people to scheme type is important. MSC figures (Fenton et al, 1984) indicate that, whilst 75 per cent of white trainees were on mode A schemes, only 59 per cent of Asians and 55 per cent of Afro-Caribbeans were on such schemes. Fenton found regional variations in these allocations with, for example, 66 per cent of Bradford's white trainees but only 42 per cent of the Asians on mode A schemes. These findings were also supported in a later study by Cross (in Cross and Smith, 1987).

In a number of studies negative views about YTS were expressed by ethnic minority respondents. This was particularly the case in the study of ethnic minority youth in Liverpool by Connolly et al (1992). Few of them were on employer led schemes and most were on schemes with poor prospects; Community Projects, Training Workshops, ITECS or college based provisions. Cross, Wrench and Barnett (1990) echo this. They found that YTS is a choice of last resort for many ethnic minority young people, particularly Asians. However, when the Asians did enter YTS they were more successful in penetrating employment related schemes than Afro-Caribbeans, who were less likely to get these 'better' schemes regardless of educational performance.

Although there is considerable evidence from these studies that ethnic minority young people are less likely than white young people to be on employer led schemes, evidence of the effect of this on the probability of obtaining employment is sparse as are comparisons between those who took up YTS places and similar individuals who did not.

Attitudes to work and to job seeking are also important factors. Ullah, Banks and Warr (1985) studied the relationship between social support, social pressures and psychological distress during unemployment in a survey of 1150 unemployed 17 year olds (776 whites and 374 Afro-Caribbean ethnic minorities). They found significant differences between the groups in some of the psychological distress variables (see also Ullah, 1985). For example, levels of depression varied between ethnic groups after a number of predictor variables such as perceived pressures and employment commitment had been controlled for (using multiple regression). The results of an earlier paper (Banks, Ullah and Warr, 1984) were interpreted to mean that ethnic minority unemployed teenagers were in better shape psychologically while unemployed as they were not as depressed or distressed as whites. The research suggested that there was some evidence of greater selectivity in job seeking by ethnic minorities. This could have been because ethnic minority young people were making a realistic appraisal of the job opportunities available to them. The Times Educational Supplement (TES, 1984), however, reported this as ethnic minoritys being 'more choosy' about jobs, a more pejorative assessment. This is a good example (as Eggleston et al suggest, 1986) of research being distorted when it is reported.

Positive attitudes to job seeking were found by Marilyn Taylor (1984) in a study of 86 young people in the Birmingham area aged 17-21 who had more than six months experience of unemployment. There were equal numbers of people of Afro-Caribbean, white and Asian origins and she concluded that there was no evidence to suggest that respondents were work shy or even that they had lost faith in the search for employment. They put a good deal of energy into the search for employment predominantly through job centres, careers offices and scanning the newspapers.

In the survey conducted by Connolly et al (1992) of Afro-Caribbean young people in Liverpool the respondents who were unemployed felt their outlook was fairly bleak; 57 per cent were only fairly hopeful and 15 per cent not at all hopeful of finding jobs. Despite this the vast majority of all respondents had hopes of establishing themselves in management or professional level employment.

Cross, Wrench and Barnett (1990) in their research found that ethnic minority young people are above average in their ambition to get jobs with training, skill and prospects, both on YTS and beyond. Asian boys and Afro-Caribbean girls are the ones with aspirations which are noticeably above their white peers. Asian girls and Afro-Caribbean boys are more likely to aspire to skilled manual employment than their peers.

In summary, the research on the attitudes of ethnic minority young people, both to unemployment and to job seeking suggest that, on the whole they were not particularly negative about these experiences, even though they often had grounds for pessimism. They also made considerable efforts to find work.

A further factor influencing an individuals employment chances is social class. Working class young people are disadvantaged by their backgrounds. They are more likely to be in families with a history of unemployment, be attending inner city schools where levels of resources may be depressed and to be entering local labour markets

46

Table 2.4: Job levels of employees, 1982

	Men			Women		
	White (%)	Afro-Caribbean (%)	Asian (%)	White (%)	Afro-Caribbean (%)	Asian (%)
Professional employer/ manager	19	5	13	7	1	5
Other non-manual	23	10	13	55	52	35
Skilled manual / manual supervisor	42	48	33	5	4	8
Semi-skilled and unskilled manual	16	35	40	32	43	51
Total	100	100	100	100	100	100

Source: Brown (1984)

Table 2.5: Job levels of men by ethnic origin in studies between 1966 and 1982 (percentages)

	Afro-Caribbean	Pakistani/(a) Bangladeshi	Indian	White
Managers[b]				
1966 West Midlands	0	1	2	12
1974 England	2	4	8	23
1982 England	5	13	-	19
Semi--Skilled and skilled manual				
1966 West Midlands	48	80(a)	51	28
1974 England	32	58	36	18
1982 England	35	40	-	16

Notes:

(a) Data for 1966 is for Pakistanis only

(b) Data for 1966 is for managers and supervisors. Date for 1974 and 1982 is for those in the professional, employer and manager group. Males aged 15-64. Data is from the three PEP/PSI Studies; Daniel (1968) and Brown (1984).

Source: Brown (1992)

offering mostly unskilled jobs, insufficient in quantity to maintain full employment.

The pattern of job levels at the beginning of the eighties is illustrated in Table 2.4 (taken from Brown 1990). Ethnic minority men and women were much less likely to be in professional jobs and much more likely to be in semi-skilled and unskilled manual jobs than their white counterparts. These differences have been remarkably persistent since the sixties even though the gap has narrowed to some extent (Table 2.5).

The Asian group is too undifferentiated a group for such an analysis though. Robinson (1988 and 1990) shows using an analysis of the Labour Force Survey that, in terms of socio-economic status the Indian group is very similar to the white group. There has historically been a sizeable group of Indian professional or white collar workers within the UK predating the peaks of labour migration in the 1950s. Robinson also analyses social mobility and finds that there have been smaller volumes of social mobility amongst the West Indian group than amongst other ethnic minority groups and mobility has been less rapid. Comparing 1971 and 1981 data from the OPCS Longitudinal Study he argues that there has been a social polarisation amongst the Indian and Pakistani communities, some individuals moving rapidly upwards into white collar work at the same time as sizeable numbers are experiencing downward mobility into unemployment. This poses an interesting question for future research and suggests that analysis should focus both on the development of a ethnic minority middle class and the problems of the less skilled and the unemployed.

The need to differentiate the Asian group is clear also when Asian Muslim women are considered. This group has, in the past had a low economic activity rate (see Brown, 1984) but a recent qualitative study has challenged some long standing stereotypes about them (Brah and Shaw, 1992). The group of young Asian women studied did not necessarily wish to work in the home as is often believed, many wanted to get good jobs with decent pay and working conditions. Most felt it was important to do paid work, both as a source of income for the family and because it gave them a measure of independence (see Wrench, 1993).

A further factor which affects the employment opportunities of both ethnic minority and white young people is the local labour market in which each individual is seeking work (see Garner, Main and Raffe, 1988). Most of the factors already considered are characteristics of individuals themselves, their qualifications for example, but these

49

qualifications may be valued differently, in terms of the jobs that can be obtained with them, depending on the structure of the local economy.

There are two separate but interrelated aspects of this; industrial divisions and regional differences. Ethnic minorities have traditionally been over represented in certain occupations and industries, in particular in manufacturing occupations. For example, the 1981 Labour Force Survey shows that 56 per cent of Afro-Caribbean men and about 50 per cent of Asian men were employed in the manufacturing and transport sectors compared with 36 per cent of white men (Eggleston et al, 1986). Manufacturing industries were in decline in the eighties and workers within them were particularly vulnerable to unemployment. New industries were, however, emerging and therefore the picture is a changing one.

In their analysis of Labour Force Survey data through the Eighties, Owen and Green (1992) suggest that 'winners' and 'losers' emerged amongst the ethnic minority population; those with manual skills in manufacturing industry suffering disproportionately from the economic changes of the decade, whilst those with non manual skills in the service sector benefited from the growth of these sectors.

These industry differences translate into regional differences also. In southern Britain in the eighties one of the key characteristics was employment in service industries and low unemployment rates. There was, by contrast, continued economic decline in areas like Manchester and Merseyside and the West Midlands was particularly hit by the decline in manufacturing industries. In such areas unemployment was not only higher than in the south but ethnic differences were larger also. By the end of the decade the unemployment rate for Pakistanis in Greater Manchester was three times the white rate and in the West Midlands Metropolitan County the unemployment rate for Pakistanis was four times the white rate (Jones, 1993). Such differences are likely to affect the employment opportunities of ethnic minority and white young people entering the labour market for the first time.

One effect that this might have (although the evidence on this is somewhat conflicting) is to discourage young people from leaving school at 16 at the earliest opportunity, the 'discouraged worker' effect (Raffe and Willms, 1989). They might prefer to stay to improve on their qualifications rather than enter a labour market where finding a job will be difficult .

The final factor of major importance is racial discrimination. This has been found to persist over time by the use of studies involving 'tester' applicants. In this method applications which were identical in terms of qualifications and experience were made by Asian, West Indian and white 'tester' applicants, the only difference being the applicants' ethnic origin. These were sent to over 100 firms in the Nottingham area and it was found that nearly half the firms interviewed the white applicants but sent rejections to ethnic minority applicants (Hubbuck and Carter, 1980). Similar results were found in a survey of 300 plants in the early Seventies (Smith 1974). Repeats of these application trials by PSI in 1984 and 1985 indicated levels of discrimination no lower than those found in 1973 and 1974 (Brown and Gay, 1985). The research, carried out in London, Birmingham and Manchester, showed that at least one third of private employers discriminated against Asian applicants, Afro-Caribbean applicants or both. The process by which ethnic minority applicants are thinned out by recruitment and selection criteria is discussed by Wrench and Lee (1983) and Jenkins (1992). It would appear from these studies that the level of employer discrimination has not markedly decreased since the early seventies.

Studies that have focused on professional occupations also suggest that racial discrimination persists here. These include studies of accountancy (CRE, 1987) and the graduate labour market (Brennan and McGeevor, 1987; Johnes and Taylor, 1989). In the latter survey which had 7812 respondents it was found that Afro-Caribbean and Asian graduates were more likely to be unemployed than their white counterparts, both six months and six years after graduation.

Racial discrimination is difficult to measure in a direct way in surveys. However, a number of authors have used model based analyses to attempt to measure the effects of direct and indirect discrimination on pay differentials. In a study of North American Indians in the Canadian Labour Market, Patrinos and Sakellariou (1991) found that, having controlled for years of schooling, years of work and other factors, the differential in earnings was due in large part to discrimination against Indians and the relatively low human capital of Indians. In a study in the UK, Pirani, Yolles and Bassa (1992) having controlled for similar factors, found that, even when ethnic minority workers had higher education and training, their wages tended to be lower when compared with their white counterparts. Tomaskovic-Devey (1992) used a model based approach to examine the characteristics that were associated with sex and race segregation in employment in US companies. This paper contains an interesting discussion of the theories that underpin the study of segregated employment structures; ideas of 'statistical discrimination' based on human capital theory that can be traced back to Becker and ideas about 'social closure' that can be traced back to Weber. Tomaskovic-Devey found in his statistical analysis of data from over seven hundred firms that larger and smaller firms were more segregated than medium sized ones and suggests reasons for this.

Summary

In this Chapter I have examined research on ethnic minority young people in education and the youth labour market, particularly focusing on research since 1980. Differences in sample design and analysis make generalisation difficult. However, it is clear that a number of factors are relevant to any comprehensive attempt to study the experiences of young people in the 16-19 age group.

In the first place a clear baseline is required for such an analysis by assessing the ethnic minority-white gap in educational attainment at 16. The review in this chapter shows that the idea of ethnic minority 'under achievement' in education is an oversimplification. Account needs to be taken of differences both between and within ethnic groups and conclusions depend on the methods of analysis used and the way in which other important factors are controlled. In a number of the studies reviewed here there was a clear limitation in the geographic scope of the sample.

In the second place the high participation rate of ethnic minority men and women in post-compulsory education is evident but the absence of a sufficiently large nationally representative sample has limited analysis about how this crucial period is used differently by ethnic minority and white young people. Any study of post-compulsory education needs to carefully follow the progress of young people through various academic and vocational routes to show more clearly how they build on their attainments at 16 and use them to move into the labour market or into higher education.

In the third place this review has shown that Afro-Caribbean and Asian young people have been less successful in establishing themselves in the youth labour market than their white counterparts. Other researchers have placed various degrees of emphasis on possible explanations for this; differing levels of attainment, routes used into the labour market, experiences on YTS, attitudes to work and job finding, social class, the effects of local labour markets and racism in the labour market. The surveys using 'tester' applicants for jobs have directly shown the extent of continuing discrimination. Other studies have been somewhat less convincing because they have not always adequately controlled for other factors. These factors need to be disentangled with a sufficiently large sample so that we can with a reasonable degree of confidence assess their relative effects. This is the task of the succeeding chapters.

3 Methodology

The data

The data for this report are drawn from the Youth Cohort Study
(YCS) of England and Wales, which is conducted in collaboration
with Social and Community Planning Research (SCPR). The YCS has
been funded, since its inception in 1984, by the Department of
Employment, the Department of Education and Science and what was
previously the Training Agency. It is a major longitudinal study of
young people's experiences as they complete their period of
compulsory education and enter the world of work, training or further
education. It covers the three years of their subsequent experiences
after they have reached the position where they are old enough to
leave school. We refer here to their first post-compulsory year of
experience as the PC1 year, their second as PC2 and their third as
PC3. Members of the sample are contacted by postal questionnaire on
three occasions and, at the end of the study, are nearly all aged 19
plus. To date, three separate cohorts have been followed up on three
separate occasions (or sweeps) at about one year intervals; the study of
a fourth and fifth cohort is in progress. In the first sweep, data is
collected on experiences up to the spring of the PC1 year. The second
sweep covers the intervening period between this and the spring of the
PC2 year. The third sweep covers the intervening period between this
and the spring of the PC3 year. (see Figure 3.1)

At the time of analysis complete data from three sweeps were
available for the first three cohorts. The analyses that follow employ
information from the second and third cohorts: those who were first in
a position to leave the educational system, if they wished, in the
summer of 1985 or the summer of 1986. It follows their experiences

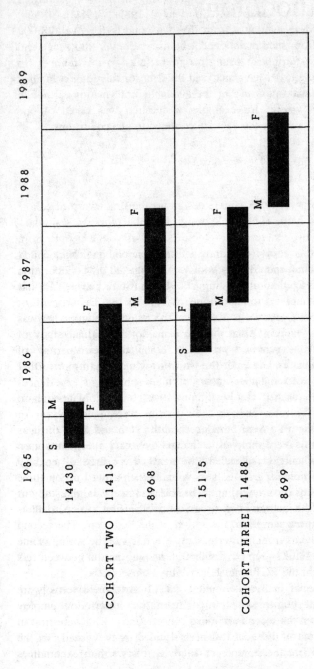

Figure 3.1 Sample design for cohorts two and three

55

through to the spring of 1988 or the spring of 1989 (for further information see, for example, Courtenay, 1989a, 1989b, 1990a, 1990b). Data were available from the two cohorts for over 28,000 young people from state maintained schools, with over 900 Asian and nearly 500 Afro-Caribbean young people included in this number. In many parts of the text I have analysed the data for this total combined group to make maximum use of the available information, although in some places where, for example, a question was asked of one cohort but not the other, the data are confined to one cohort only.

Sample design

The cohort two, sweep one sample design for the first sweep of cohort two is described here. The sample design for cohort three was similar.

The cohort two, sweep one sample is one of young people from state maintained schools (excluding special schools) in England and Wales who reached minimum school leaving age in 1984-1985. That is, they were all aged 16 on 31 August 1986 and were between 16 and 17 when they completed the questionnaire booklet.

The sample was selected as follows. DES listed all eligible schools in England (the Welsh Office did the same for Wales) having first ordered schools by school type within Local Education Authority (LEA) and region. The data for this stratification came from the DES form 7 exercise carried out in January each year.

A 10% sample of eligible pupils was selected within each participating school by including those who were aged 16 on 31 August 1985 and who were born on the 5th, 15th and 25th of each month. The pupils were sampled in January-February 1985 when they were still at school. Headteachers were asked by DES to consult pupils about participating in the survey and they passed to SCPR the names of pupils who were willing to be included in the sample. At the time the pupils' names were collected no final decision had been taken about the size of the sample.

SCPR received from DES a sample of 2,423 schools which accounted for 41,087 pupils. Table 3.1 shows that the sample of pupils received by SCPR matched very closely the population estimates of pupils in the different types of maintained schools in England. Welsh pupils are omitted from the comparison as the population figures were not available.

By the autumn of 1985, it had been decided by the Youth Cohort Steering Group (made up of representatives from the three funding departments, Sheffield Careers Service, SCPR and Sheffield University) that the issued sample for the second cohort should be twenty-thousand. SCPR therefore randomly deleted pupils (but not schools) from the received sample. The sample so selected was 19,933, that is, approximately one pupil in two. The random deletion of pupils to yield a sample of around twenty thousand led to a reduction of seven schools from the sample (small schools having 'lost' all of their eligible pupils). A further six schools which were selected were subsequently omitted from the sample either because no addresses had been provided for selected pupils or because pupils with the wrong birthdates had been selected. The final productive sample (that is of actual respondents) was made up of 14,430 pupils from 2,377 schools.

For the second sweep of this cohort a separate sample of independent school pupils was introduced but these pupils were excluded from my study. Independent school pupils were sampled at each sweep of cohort three also but, again, these were excluded from our analysis. The sample design for cohort three was similar to that of the previous cohort except that a 20% sample of eligible pupils was selected within each participating school; this sample was therefore somewhat more clustered than the previous ones.

Weighting

Weighting of the data was carried out on the basis of certain characteristics (gender, region, school type, stayer/leaver and attainment group) known to be associated with non response using population data provided by the DES in order to allow for differential response. All the analyses we report use the weighted figures.

In Cohort Two actual attainment categories were provided by DES in respect of sample members who were known (by DES) to have left school. The definition of a 'leaver' was that used in the DES School Leavers' Survey and included not only those who had left full-time education but others, for example those going on to tertiary colleges and other further education establishments. SCPR 'matched' the names of those for whom attainment was provided with sample members. Attainment data, where available (that is for school 'leavers') were added to the data tape so that weighting could take account of attainment as well as sex, school type and region.

Table 3.1: Comparison of cohort two sweep one sample with population estimates provided by DES*

	Population		Received from DES	Selected by SCPR
	No	%	%	%
Sixth form college	1,891	0	0	0
Up-to-16 comprehensives	193,606	29	30	30
Up-to18 comprehensives	408,002	62	61	61
Grammar	18,052	3	2	2
Modern	36,162	5	5	5
Other	5,209	1	1	1
Base:	662,922	(100)	38,374	18,708

Notes:* The population estimates were provided by DES for "all pupils aged 15 on 31 August 1984"; data collected in January 1985. The table refers to England only since DES could not provide population estimates for Wales. Excludes Independent schools.

The grossing factors (weights) were chosen so that the total number in the weighted sample should be as close an approximation as practicable to the unweighted sample size.

In cohort three it was necessary to adopt a somewhat different weighting strategy from that described above. The sample design for cohort three involved a greater degree of clustering within schools than had been the case in the previous cohorts. This had an unforeseen effect on the weighting scheme. The attainment data used as one of the weighting factors was only collected by DES for those born on 5th, 15th and 25th of each month (i.e. for a ten per cent sample). Cohort three involved a twenty per cent sample within schools (i.e. it included also those born on 10th, 20th and 30th of each month). Therefore only half the necessary attainment data was available. The solution adopted for this problem was to use weights derived from self reported attainment and self reported stayer/leaver data from cohort two. Although the data used for this was thus one year out of date it is believed that the effect of this would be small as such estimates are fairly stable over time.

The above weighting scheme was developed by SCPR. Further weighting was necessary in my study in order to combine cohorts two and three, the sample size for cohort two being different from that of cohort three. Weights were derived here on the assumption that the populations from which each of the cohort samples were drawn were both of equal size.

Question design

The questionnaire not surprisingly, tended to reflect the interests of the three commissioning departments. The Department of Education and Science is particularly interested in participation and performance in post-compulsory education. The Department of Employment is interested in the industries and occupations young people enter, the rate of job changing, how jobs are obtained and unemployment. The Training Agency (as it was then called) was interested in the Youth Training Scheme and the transfer from this into full-time employment.

One of the pivotal questions of the survey, used at each sweep, asked about the respondents' activities for each month since the previous sweep; whether they had been in full-time education, in a job, on YTS, out of work or doing something else. This came to be known as the diary question. At each sweep detailed questions were then asked about an individual's current activity. This data was then used in a number of ways. In the first place it was used to provide a cross sectional view of, say, labour market activities or educational attainment at any particular stage, at age 16 or age 19 for example. In the second place it was used to chart an individual's progress over the survey period, by making use of the longitudinal nature of the survey; for example by showing the way additional academic or vocational qualifications were gained. In the third place, and perhaps most interestingly, I was able to construct a typology of routes into the labour market which cut across a static view of labour market activities at one point in time. Individuals may have spent time on a YTS scheme but not necessarily immediately on leaving school at 16. Those who used YTS as a route whenever they did this could, for some purposes, best be considered together. Other individuals may have taken A levels with a view to continuing into higher education; but they may have taken this route immediately at 16 or first stayed on at school or college for an extra year to improve their O level

59

qualifications. Those individuals aiming for A levels were grouped together for some of the analysis. The detailed information available in the survey enabled such routes to be identified and distinguished and are an important addition to the cross sectional method of analysis.

The completeness of this diary data is a major strength of the YCS. In a small number of other areas the data were less complete and therefore of more limited value. For example, in the section on YTS respondents were asked what, if anything, they liked most or disliked most about the scheme. This was an open ended question, no response categories were given, and the difficulties of coding this data coupled with a high non response meant that the question was of limited usefulness.

There was a general issue about combining responses from two separate cohorts of the survey. The questionnaires from cohort two and cohort three were quite similar but there were differences in question order and coding. Considerable computing and recoding was therefore necessary not only to merge the three sweeps of each cohort but to amalgamate the questions from the two cohorts.

Three other major question areas need to be discussed; the data on examination achievements, the way in which ethnic groups were defined and the way in which socio-economic background was treated.

Data on examination achievements were collected at each sweep of YCS. Details of fifth year examination results were collected during the first sweep. For each subject, respondents were asked to report whether they studied for an O level, CSE or 16 plus exam, as well as for the grade they received in each. It was possible to compare the information the sample provided both with national estimates of the aggregated distributions of examination achievements and also with the results obtained by individual school leavers. Although in the latter case there were examples of discrepancies, no systematic differences emerged; sometimes respondents 'over reported' their results, sometimes they 'under reported' them (possibly in the latter case because they failed to collect their results). In general terms, however, the match was good, both in terms of the aggregated and the individual level data. As a consequence, we have here a data base on individual respondents' exam performances which was flexible, wide-ranging and lent itself to the construction of various summary statistics.

In the analysis of examination results in the post 16 compulsory period it was necessary to distinguish between academic and vocational qualifications. Getting some purchase on the underlying structures of post 16 educational provision is far from straightforward. There are many different types of course that can be taken and responsibility for their delivery is entrusted to a number of different agencies and educational institutions.

From the detailed information available on the courses and qualifications young people pursued I constructed a five fold classification of the major courses they were taking. 'Two or more A levels' was an obvious cut off point for those studying during the post-compulsory years with an eye on entry to some form of higher education. Three other groupings also suggested themselves, 'National Vocational Level 3 Qualifications' (NVQ Level 3) such as BTEC National Certificates, 'National Vocational Level 1 and 2 Qualifications' (NVQ Levels 1, 2) and 'Four or more O levels'.

In an earlier analysis of Youth Cohort Study data it was shown that there was relatively little mixing of academic subjects (i.e. A levels and O levels) and vocational subjects (see Gray and Pattie, 1988). However, it was found that some decisions did need to be made at the margins about which courses the study programmes of particular young people were mainly directed at. There was also a group from whom it was only possible to establish that some 'other course' was pursued which did not fit into any of the above four categories; in these cases individuals were assigned, wherever possible, to the courses which were most likely to represent the major thrust of their education at this stage.

In all studies of this kind there is a problem in determining both the classification categories and the terminology to be used to describe ethnic groups. The debate about this has continued for some time. There was considerable discussion about the possible inclusion of an ethnic question in the 1981 Population Census and the form such a question should take (Sillitoe, 1978; Booth, 1988). This debate still continues (Mason 1990) and it is agreed that no one set of categories is capable of serving all aspects of the analysis of ethnic relations. A question on ethnic origin was piloted and used in the 1991 Population Census after considerable discussion.

In the YCS respondents were asked to answer the following question: 'Please tell us which of the following ethnic groups you belong to. Your answer will help us to know how equal opportunities policies are working'. The answer categories offered were: /African/Caribbean origin; Indian origin; Pakistani origin; Bangladeshi origin; White; None of these; I prefer not to say. For the purposes of the analysis the first group was described as Afro-Caribbean and the Indian, Pakistani and Bangladeshi groups were

61

described as Asian. The Afro-Caribbean and Asian groups are sometimes collectively described as black. This practice follows that adopted by the Commission for Racial Equality in 1984 based on the view that this collective term best describes those individuals who are most likely to be the victims of racial discrimination and highlights their shared experiences.

There is some disagreement, though, about the appropriateness of this. Modood, (1988) argues that the term black requires Asians to subordinate their own identity to one forged by people of Afro descent. He suggests that the term 'ethnic minority and Asian' is also unsuitable because it continues to imply Afro leadership whereas, in numerical terms the second group is more important than the first. The problem is that finding an acceptable alternative is difficult. The term 'ethnic minorities' leads to problems because there are a number of groups and communities in Britain who are technically ethnic minorities but who are not, by any definition black. Mason suggests that a term which could be appropriate because it describes people who may be the objects of racism is 'people who are not white'. This seems to be a rather cumbersome description and one unlikely to be used in practice so we have reverted to the more common term 'ethnic minority' realising its limitations.

A further issue here is the way individuals responded to the ethnic question and whether they themselves had difficulties with it. This issue is discussed in the next section.

In order to derive socio-economic groups the Registrar General's classification was used. Respondents were asked to provide information about the occupations of the parents in whose household they were living (father/mother/stepfather/stepmother as appropriate). This information was then coded into the seventeenfold classification of socio-economic groups provided by the Registrar-General. These 17 groups were then collapsed into three broader ones: professional/managerial, intermediate and manual. The professional/managerial group was made up of the socio-economic groups 1, 2 ,3, 4, 13 and 14 and includes farmers. The intermediate group combines groups 5, 6, 7 and 12, i.e. intermediate and junior nonmanual workers, personal service workers and some selfemployed (own account workers other than professionals). The manual group contains all manual workers, skilled, semi-skilled and unskilled. Those in the Armed Forces and others who were inadequately described have been excluded from these groupings.

Data on social background is often incomplete in surveys of this kind and this survey is no exception. About one in five respondents

Data on social background is often incomplete in surveys of this kind and this survey is no exception. About one in five respondents did not provide information about their father's occupation in a way that permitted them to be assigned to a socio-economic group. Where this information was missing (for whatever reason) and information was available on the mother's occupation, this was substituted. This procedure reduced the number of cases where information was missing to about one in eight. Since occupations reported for women were less likely to fall in the professional/managerial group, this procedure had the effect of slightly reducing the overall percentages in the sample in this group. There was also more missing data on fathers' occupation amongst Afro-Caribbean respondents.

The description of young people's social background available to us is a fairly broad one and the data, as coded, do not lend themselves to more fine-grained analyses. More complex coding procedures are being operationalized on subsequent YCS surveys.

Response

The strength of this analysis is that it is based on a very large nationally representative sample. Even with such a large sample, however, non response bias may still, potentially be a problem.

The overall response rates for this survey, compared with other postal surveys, is in general high, running at between 70 and 80 per cent for each sweep. (Table 3.2). The response rate for cohort two, sweep one was 72% and the reasons for non response are shown in Table 3.3. A small number of individuals were ineligible because their birth dates fell outside the required days of the month and a small number of questionnaires were returned by the post office. For the majority of non response, however, the reasons were not known.

Table 3.2: Response rates for both cohorts

	Cohort 2		Cohort 3	
	No. of cases	Response rate (%)	No. of cases	Response rate (%)
Sample selected	19,988		19,684	
Sweep one	14,430	72	15,115	77
Sweep two	11,413	79	11,488	76
Sweep three	8,968	79	8,699	76

Notes:* Excludes Independent schools

Table 3.3: Reasons for non-response in cohort two, sweep one (C2S1)

	No. of cases	%	%
1. **Selected by SCPR from DES sample**	19,988	(100)	
not mailed by SCPR			
- ineligible - birthday outside cohort year or not born on 5, 15, 25 or month	257	1	
- no address given	142	1	
- inadequate address	17	*	
- refusal in advance	6	*	
- known to have died	1	*	
2. **Mailed by SCPR**	19,565	98	(100)

3. Non-response:		
- returned by the post office	210	1	1
- refusal by respondent or on his/her behalf	186	1	1
- respondent had gone away	12	*	*
- respondent died	2	*	*
- respondent too ill to take part	1	*	*
	4,674	23	24
4. Withdrawn at clerical edit (incomplete, 'spoiled')	50	*	*
5. Productive questionnaires	14,430	72	74

Notes:

The symbol * denotes a non-zero quantity of less than 0.5%.

Source: Courtenay (1989a)

A further question is that of differential non response for ethnic minority young people. The number of respondents who did not answer the ethnic question was small (2%) as was the number whose answer to this question was '

I prefer not to say' (2%). We looked for other sources with which to establish the representativeness of our respondents with respect to ethnic background. Of the very limited options available the Labour Force Survey (LFS) seemed most satisfactory, and a reworking of the data available from that source suggested rather similar proportions (see Table 3.4). In both studies the proportions of respondents who were white was comparable (at approx. 95 per cent) as were the proportions who were Afro-Caribbean or Asian.

This finding is reassuring coupled with the fact that weighting the data using characteristics known to having been associated with non response will have reduced the effect of non response. There is some evidence though that, after the weighting exercise has been conducted, non response is still slightly higher for the Afro-Caribbean group than for the others. In cohort three, for example, there was greater attrition in the Afro-Caribbean group between sweep one and sweep three, compared with other groups.

The effect of this is not exactly clear but if, for example, it is the low attaining Afro-Caribbean groups which are not responding, this means our results will overstate examination success and probably understate unemployment rates. The picture offered by the YCS probably errs on the optimistic side when it comes to looking at the experience of ethnic minority groups.

Analysis

The analysis that was carried out is described in detail in the chapters which follow. A few overall general comments which apply to a number of the sections are useful here, however.

Whilst the focus of this research is on the Afro-Caribbean and Asian groups, it is important to emphasise that as a basis for analysis this categorisation is necessarily an oversimplified one. The range of experiences within the groups is large; the groups are not homogeneous in terms of culture, country of parents' origin, social class, previous educational experiences or aspirations. It is possible to make some of these differences explicit by controlling for them in the analysis, but with many other differences this is just not possible due to the size of the sample or unmeasured variables.

The term Asian, in particular, is used to describe a number of different groups (Bangladeshi, Pakistani, Indian, etc). The job levels of these groups has been found in recent surveys (Brown 1984) to be very different. Members of the Bangladeshi group, for example, are much less likely than others to be in skilled non-manual jobs and more likely to be in semi-skilled or unskilled work. There has similarly been a tendency for some education researchers to ignore the heterogeneity of the Asian group and focus on the educational attainments of the Afro-Caribbean group. Data from the Inner London Education Authority (Byford and Mortimore, 1985 and ILEA, 1990) however have shown that the mean examination performances of the Bangladeshi and Turkish pupils have consistently been lower than that of Afro-Caribbean pupils.

Table 3.4: Comparison of the proportions of young people from particular ethnic origins in the Youth Cohort Study (C2S1) and the Labour Force Survey

Ethnic Origin[a]	Youth Cohort Study (C2S1) %	Labour Force Survey[b] %
White	94.9	95.4
Afro-Caribbean	1.8	1.8
Asian (Indian, Pakistani or Bangladeshi)	3.3	2.8
Total	100.0	100.0
Numbers of cases	13,348.0	11,560.0

Notes:

(a) There are always difficulties in comparing the size of ethnic groups differences in surveys when slightly different questions have been asked of respondents. The groups listed here are those for which comparisons are most easily made. Respondents in YCS were asked to answer the following questions: 'Please tell us which of the following ethnic groups you belong to. Your answer will help us to know how equal opportunities policies are working'. The answer categories offered were 'Black/African/Caribbean origin; Indian origin, Pakistani origin, Bangladeshi origin;White; None of these; I prefer not to say'.

(b) Source: C. Shaw (1988) 'Latest estimates of ethnic minority populations: Great Britain 1984-6', in Population Trends, 1988. The numbers in the age group 16-29 have been used.

A similar problem faced us with an analysis of gender differences. Questions about whether, for example, Afro-Caribbean girls make better progress than Afro-Caribbean boys are clearly important but small sample sizes sometimes meant that such analyses were not always possible. Males and females were combined in the analysis only where the sample size was small or the tables were complex.

Logit models have been used in a number of places in the analyses that follow. Their strength is that they go beyond comparison of pairs of variables and enable us to investigate the effects of a number of factors taken together. Logit models also enable us to focus on discrimination. Discrimination, by its covert nature, is difficult to assess in quantitative studies but analyses which control for a whole series of other variables and then still find ethnic differences provide some evidence of discrimination taking place.

Mention should be made here of terminology used in the study. It should be borne in mind that when we refer to '16 year olds' in this report, this is a shorthand description for the age group who represent a year cohort passing through the school system, that is the group in the first post-compulsory year. Similarly when we refer to '19 year olds' we mean young people in the third year since the end of their compulsory period of schooling, again they may differ in age by up to twelve months across the group.

Summary

The Youth Cohort Study of England and Wales is a nationally representative sample survey funded by three government departments since 1984. It is based on a two stage sample with schools as the first stage units. Although the questionnaires for cohorts two and three were somewhat different it was possible after computing and recoding to combine the results of these two cohorts to produce a sample of 28,000 young people with over 900 Asian and about 500 Afro-Caribbean respondents. Independent schools were excluded from this analysis. Postal questionnaires were sent to the respondents on three separate occasions (three sweeps) over a 30 month period covering the age range 16-19 . A key question was about employment status for each month over the whole period (the diary question). Detailed data was collected at each sweep about examination results. The ethnic question was a self report question and data on socio-economic status was collected using the Registrar General's classification. Although there was some survey attrition over the three sweeps of the study the response rate at each sweep was high.

As a result, the Youth Cohort Study provides a set of data which is the strongest and most reliable of its kind in England and Wales and enables detailed analysis to be carried out of the progress of young people, either through post-compulsory education, or into the labour market.

4 Home and school at 16

Introduction

This chapter has two parts. The first part is about the home and family background of the respondents and the second part is about examination results at 16, in the fifth year of secondary school. Both of these form an important backdrop to the choices made at 16 and the decision about whether to continue in post-compulsory education or to enter the labour market.

Home background

The family background factors are illustrated in Table 4.1. Whatever success was achieved by the young people themselves, it is clear that they set off from different starting points. The fathers of ethnic minority young people were much less likely to be in a full-time job and two or three times more likely to be unemployed than similar whites, with the consequent loss of income involved. Whilst for the fathers of white respondents 9 per cent were unemployed, for Afro-Caribbeans 14 per cent were unemployed and for Asians 26 per cent were unemployed.

It is interesting to note the particularly high unemployment rates for Asians and this is likely to be due to particularly high unemployment amongst the Pakistani and Bangladeshi group (see the discussion in Chapter Two). The mothers of Afro-Caribbean young people were more likely than others to be working full-time but probably in low paid jobs. The mothers of Asian young people were much more likely to be economically inactive and working in the home than the mothers of other young people. It is likely that the overall Asian figure hides a large difference between Muslim women and other women of Asian origin; for Muslim women the economic activity rate is particularly low (only 18 per cent in the PSI study, Brown 1984).

The social backgrounds of the three groups also differed markedly. Whilst less than one in ten of those of Afro-Caribbean and Asian background were to be found in the professional group, this compares with about one in five for the white group. Conversely, about six out of ten of the Afro-Caribbean and Asian groups were to be found in the manual category compared with fewer than five out of ten of the white group.

The pattern of housing tenure follows that found in similar surveys. The Afro-Caribbean group was more likely than the white group to be renting, either from the local authority or privately, and the Asian group was more likely than the white group to be in owner occupied housing. This should not be taken to mean that the Asian households were more affluent; owner occupation amongst Asians is high amongst all socio-economic groups (Brown, 1984). The ethnic minority group, as a whole, was also three times as likely to be living in the inner city compared with the white group (table not shown).

Such comparisons enable us to place the labour market transitions of these young people in some kind of context. The picture is an overall one, however, and conceals considerable variations in material circumstances. It also shows, in common with many other studies, that on average the material circumstances of ethnic minority households are poorer than those of white households.

Examination achievements

The respondents gave details of their fifth year examination results during the first sweep of the cohort. Here, in the first instance, results are presented for the respondents to cohort two. For each subject, they were asked to report whether they studied for an O level, CSE or 16 plus exam, as well as the grade they received in each. The examination data was validated firstly by comparison with national estimates provided by DES and secondly by comparison with results provided by DES for the individuals included in the sample. This process is described more fully in the previous chapter. Table 4.2 and Figure 4.1 provide the results from an analysis of this data.

71

Table 4.1: The respondents' home background by ethnic origin (percentages)

	Afro-Caribbean (%)	Asian (%)	White (%)	None of these (%)	All (%)
a) Father's employment status					
Full-time job	68	62	83	79	83
Part-time job	1	1	1	1	1
Unemployed	14	26	9	12	10
Retired	5	5	3	4	3
Other	12	6	4	4	3
Total	100	100	100	100	100
b) Mother's employment status					
Full-time job	49	28	30	27	30
Part-time job	24	7	37	31	35
Unemployed	8	10	4	7	5
Retired	1	1	1	1	1
Housework	16	53	26	30	27
Other	2	1	2	4	1
Total	100	100	100	100	100

c) **Household social class**

Professional	8	9	21	17	20
Intermediate	31	32	32	35	32
Manual	62	60	47	47	47
Total	101	101	100	99	99

d) **Housing tenure**

Renting	40	16	28	44	29
Owner occupied	60	84	72	56	71
Total	100	100	100	100	100

No. of cases	483	910	26,082	985	28,460

Base: All respondents

73

Differences in exam results between groups

Three different measures of fifth year examination results are presented in Table 4.2. For each one, there is a rather similar pattern. Young people from white backgrounds reported the highest results; the gap between them and the Asian group was mostly rather small. On the other hand, the gap between those two groups and the Afro-Caribbean group was rather larger. This general pattern is confirmed by the results reported in Figure 4.1. Just over one in five (21 per cent) whites and just under one in five (19 per cent) Asians had achieved five or more 'higher-grade' passes compared with fewer than one in ten (7 per cent) Afro-Caribbeans.

Table 4.2: Fifth year examination results by ethnic origin

	Ave. No. Higher Grade Passes	Ave. No. Passes Any Grade	Ave. Exam Score[a]	No. of Cases
Afro-Caribbean	1.09 (1.92)[b]	5.07 (2.80)	16.6 (12.3)	244
Asian	1.93 (2.73)	5.67 (2.87)	21.1 (15.4)	435
White	2.15 (2.83)	5.70 (3.03)	22.1 (16.0)	12,669
All	2.12 (2.82)	5.69 (3.03)	22.0 (15.9)	13,448

Base: Respondents in Cohort 2

Notes:
(a) This exam score is based on a scoring system first developed by researchers at the ILEA. O-level grades receive the following points: A=7, B=6, C=5, D=4, E=3. CSE grades: grade 1 = 5, grade 2=4, grade 5=1. Ungraded results are scored at zero. (see Byford and Mortimore, 1985).
(b) The figures in brackets show the standard deviations for each average.

By concentrating on the higher levels of exam achievement, however, it is possible to exaggerate the extent of the differences. Expressing the differences in Table 4.2 in a common metric, they amount to between one fifth and one third of a standard deviation, depending on which particular summary measure of exam achievement is employed. Standard deviations of this magnitude suggest a considerable degree of overlap in the scores of the groups, and this impression is borne out by the distributions of the three groups' exam scores in Figure 4.2; they do indeed overlap to a considerable extent.

The finding that young people from professional/managerial backgrounds do better in terms of public examinations is well established and is supported by the data presented in Figure 4.3. There was somewhat less overlap between the three socio-economic groups in comparison with the differences related to ethnic background.

Small differences associated with gender also emerged in the data, with females slightly out performing males (figure not shown).

In Table 4.3 I have combined the information relating to socio-economic grouping, ethnic background and gender. Amongst all three ethnic groups those from professional/managerial backgrounds scored highest and those from the manual groups lowest. The socio-economic group coded as 'other' were all respondents who did not provide sufficient information for their grouping to be established. About two out of ten Afro-Caribbeans and three out of ten Asians fell into this group compared with about one out of ten of the white group. The 'other' group tended to score rather lower than the remaining socio-economic group.

With respect to gender differences, the exam scores of white females were significantly superior to those of white males but for the other two ethnic groups the differences between the sexes were small or not significant.

Looking at the lower half of Table 4.3 (which rearranges the information in the top half of the table) there were small differences between those from the different ethnic backgrounds. Careful attention needs to be paid, however, to the numbers of respondents on which some of these estimates are based, especially in the professional/managerial grouping. Perhaps the most noteworthy finding to emerge from these analyses, however, is the relatively high performance of young people of Asian origin (and notably males) in the intermediate and manual socio-economic groups, both in comparison with whites and Afro-Caribbeans.

An analysis of variance was carried out using exam scores as the dependent variable and gender, socio-economic group and ethnic origin as potentially significant 'explanatory' factors. To what extent could these three factors alone account for differences in young people's exam performance?

Two inferences can be drawn from this analysis (see Table 4.4). First, all three factors were found to be statistically associated with exam scores but, of the three, that relating to socio-economic group

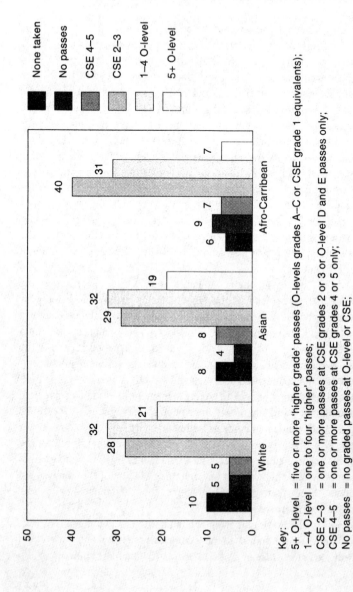

Key:

5+ O-level = five or more 'higher grade' passes (O-levels grades A–C or CSE grade 1 equivalents);

1–4 O-level = one to four 'higher' passes;

CSE 2–3 = one or more passes at CSE grades 2 or 3 or O-level D and E passes only;

CSE 4–5 = one or more passes at CSE grades 4 or 5 only;

No passes = no graded passes at O-level or CSE;

None = no O-level or CSE examinations

Figure 4.1 Fifth year examination results: percentages reaching specified levels by ethnic origin

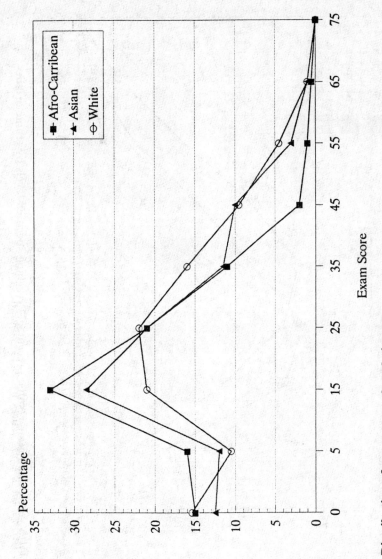

Figure 4.2 Distribution of exam scores by ethnic group

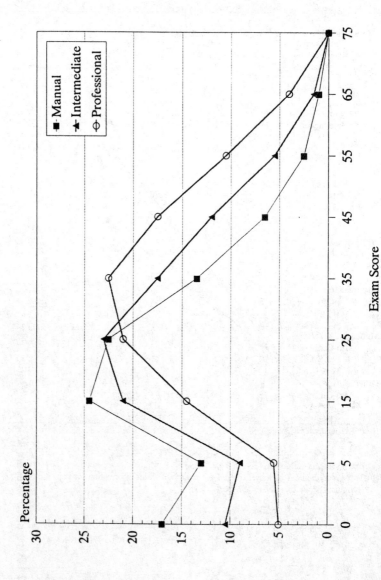

Figure 4.3 Distribution of exam scores by socio-economic group

Table 4.3: Average exam score[a], by ethnic origin, sex and socio-economic group

	Average exam score		No of cases	Standard deviation of exam scores	
	Male	Female		Male	Female
Afro-Caribbean					
Professional	27.1	24.9	12	7.5	8.2
Intermediate	21.1	18.1	68	13.5	11.9
Manual	14.3	15.6	115	11.6	12.5
Other[b]	12.1	16.1	49	11.5	11.1
All	(16.4)	(16.8)	(244)	(12.7)	(12.1)
Asian:					
Professional	30.7	27.8	17	23.2	16.0
Intermediate	27.2	25.9	95	14.2	16.3
Manual	23.3	22.5	189	16.6	13.9
Other	12.9	14.1	133	11.0	11.4
All	(21.2)	(20.9)	(435)	(16.0)	(14.7)
White:					
Professional	30.4	32.3	2,118	16.7	15.7
Intermediate	23.7	25.6	3,903	16.2	15.3
Manual	17.6	20.6	5,218	14.2	14.5
Other	13.0	13.4	1,430	14.0	13.4
All	(20.9)	(23.4)	(12,669)	(16.1)	(15.8)
Professional:					
Afro-Caribbean	27.1	24.9	12		
Asian	30.7	27.8	17		
White	30.4	32.3	2,118		
Intermediate:					
Afro-Caribbean	21.1	18.1	68		
Asian	27.2	25.9	95		
White	23.7	25.0	3,903		
Manual:					
Afro-Caribbean	14.3	15.6	115		
Asian	23.3	22.5	189		
White	17.6	20.0	5,218		
Other:					
Afro-Caribbean	12.1	16.1	49		
Asian	12.9	14.1	133		
White	13.0	13.4	1,430		

Base: Respondents in Cohort 2

Note:
(a) Exam score as defined in Table 4.2
(b) This group includes all those who did not report sufficient information for their socio-economic grouping to be established.

Table 4.4: Examination scores[a]: analysis of variance

	Sum of Squares	df	Significance of F
Main effects[b]:			
Sex	14,449	1	0.000
Ethnic Origin	5,319	2	0.000
Socio-economic group	379,342	2	0.000
Two-way interactions:			
Sex and ethnic origin	735	2	0.194
Sex and socio-economic group	1,725	3	0.053
Ethnic origin and socio-economic group	2,466	6	0.088
Three-way interactions:			
Sex, ethnic origin and socio-economic group	892	6	0.679
Residual	2,981,769	13,324	
Total	3,392,569	13,347	

Base: Respondents in Cohort 2

Note:
(a) Exam score as defined in Table 4.2
(b) Given the non-orthogonality of the design, the sum of squares attributed to socio-economic group represents the variation accounted for by this term taking account of sex and ethnic origin.

accounted for by far the largest part of the total variance that could be explained. Secondly, the larger part of the variance in exam scores remained unexplained by these three factors by themselves.

It would be tempting to conclude, from these analyses, that socio-economic background was a far more important source of variation in young people's exam scores than gender or ethnic origin. Certainly, in this analysis socio-economic group explained more of the variability than the other two factors. However, as Plewis (1987) has noted, statistical attempts to 'control for' social background are not without difficulty. The measures that are usually employed are coarse grained ones and may well conceal other real differences such as living conditions. Making the measures less coarse grained would, of course, probably make them better predictors of achievement. Similar considerations apply in the present case. Furthermore, the ethnic origin of young people's parents may well have affected the kind of employment their parents subsequently obtained and hence their parents' socio-economic grouping in our classification.

Results for combined cohorts

The preceding analysis was carried out using cohort two data only. The results for cohorts two and three combined are given in Table 4.5. These show similar results to those in Table 4.2 and Figure 4.1. The contrasts were starkest when the average number of 'higher grade' passes was compared. Whites did about twice as well as Afro-Caribbeans on average, but on all measures Asians came fairly close to whites. A fairly similar story emerges in terms of percentages who obtained 4 or more 'higher grades'. It was decided to focus on this group as an appropriate group for future analysis as individuals in this cluster were those who were very likely to continue into post-compulsory education. Whilst one in four whites and Asians fall into this category only one in ten Afro-Caribbeans do so. By concentrating on the highest levels of achievement only the extent to which there are similarities may be unintentionally ignored. For example, if the proportions gaining one or more higher grade passes are compared, then the white advantage is by no means as marked. A similar picture emerges from the use of the average exam score. In both these latter cases whites were doing about a third better than Afro-Caribbeans, rather than twice as well. It is clear, in other words, that statements about the extent of differences in achievement are, to some extent, dependent on the summary measures employed to assess them.

Comparisons with earlier surveys

The results of previous studies of examination achievements has already been discussed in Chapter Two. The results of our analyses are added to these in Table 4.6. The results all relate to fifth year examination performances with the exception of studies numbers 3 and 4 which were based on DES School Leaver's Statistics.

81

Table 4.5: Fifth year examination results by ethnic origin and gender

| | Ave. No. higher grade passes | Ave. exam score* | No. of higher grade passes | | | Total | No. of cases |
			0 (%)	1-3 (%)	4+ (%)	(%)	
Afro-Caribbean							
Male	1.1	15.5	62	27	11	100	227
Female	1.2	17.0	58	30	12	100	256
All	1.1	16.3	60	29	11	100	483
Asian							
Male	2.1	21.3	50	25	25	100	526
Female	1.8	21.4	49	29	22	100	384
All	1.9	21.4	50	26	24	100	910
White							
Male	2.0	21.1	50	25	25	100	13,134
Female	2.3	23.4	44	28	28	100	12,949
All	2.2	22.2	47	27	26	100	26,082

82

None of these

Male	1.1	14.6	66	22	12	100	471
Female	1.4	17.3	58	28	14	100	514
All	1.2	16.0	62	25	13	100	985
All	2.1	21.9	48	27	25	100	28,460

Base: All respondents

Note:
* Exam score as defined in Table 4.2.

83

Table 4.6: Exam results by ethnic origin: a comparison of the results from six surveys[a]

Study, location and year of exam results [b]	No. Exam Taken (%)	No. Graded Passes (%)	1+ CSE 4/5 (%)	1+ CSE 2/3 (%)	1-4 O Lev (%)	5+ O Lev (%)	Total (%)	No. of Cases
Afro-Caribbean								
1) London 1972[b]	(——17——)		18	44	20	0	100	250
2) Inner London, 1976	11	7	20	40	21	2	100	2,382
3) 6 LEAs, 1979	(——17——)		(——80——)			3	100	718
4) 5 LEAs, 1982	(——19——)		(——75——)			6	100	653
5) Inner London, 1985	14	3	13	38	27	5	100	2,981
6) YCS (C2S1), 1985	6	9	7	40	31	7	100	244
Asian								
1) London, 1972	Not available							
2) Inner London, 1976	14	3	8	29	27	17	100	389
3) 6 LEAs, 1979	(——20——)		(——63——)			17	100	466
4) 5 LEAs, 1982	(——19——)		(——64——)			17	100	571
5) Inner London, 1985	16	2	8	26	30	18	100	1,124
6) YCS (C2S1), 1985	8	4	8	29	32	19	100	435

Total sample (all pupils) (c)

1) London, 1972	(----30----)		12	31	23	3	100	2,018
2) Inner London, 1976	19	8	11	27	26	10	100	24,398
3) 6 LEAs, 1979	(----21----)		(----64----)			15	100	6,196
4) 5 LEAs, 1982	(----19----)		(----63----)			18	100	5,942
5) Inner London, 1985	19	3	9	29	30	10	100	17,058
6) YCS (C2S1), 1985	10	5	5	28	31	20	100	14,429

Note:
(a) Fuller details of the studies may be found in the references as follows: (1) Maughan and Rutter (1986); (2) Mabey (1986); (3) and (4) Department of Education & Science (1985), one LEA dropped out of the later survey; (5) Kysel (1988) and (6) present study.

(b) The year referred to here is that in which the exams were taken. Publications sometimes followed several years later.

(c) Includes Afro-Caribbean, Asian, white and other ethnic groups.

In certain respects, my findings parallel those of these earlier studies. I found few differences in the average exam results between Asian and White students and the results for Afro-Caribbeans were, on average, somewhat lower. This was most noticeable in terms of the proportions reaching the higher levels of exam achievement.

This evidence differed from that obtained in previous studies in two important respects. First, this data reveal little evidence of gender-related differences within ethnic minority groups; Tomlinson (1983) in her review reports better results for Afro-Caribbean girls compared with boys. Secondly, this data provide the highest estimates of the proportions of Afro-Caribbean young people obtaining one or more 'higher grade' passes reported to date. This may be, in part, because of general improvements in the standards reached by the school population at large, and the Afro-Caribbean group in particular. At the same time, however, my review of these other studies suggests that they may have offered a somewhat depressed picture of the absolute standards being reached by the various ethnic groups by virtue of adopting sampling procedures which focused on inner city and other relatively disadvantaged communities. In contrast, this study has drawn upon a nationally representative sample. However, the relative position of Afro-Caribbean young people in comparison with the whole sample would not appear to have changed much over this 12 year period.

Summary

The data presented here confirm many of the findings of previous researchers. In particular, they reveal differences associated with ethnic background. But the analyses we have undertaken also reveal very considerable within-group differences; by merely focusing on average differences between groups, the considerable overlaps between them have tended to be obscured. At the same time the traditional concentration on the 'high hurdle' of five or more O level (or equivalent) passes has accentuated this general perception, especially for Afro-Caribbean young people, by focusing on one comparative extreme of the statistical distribution. Approaches which provide better descriptions of the variability that exists, both between and within groups, seem important.

These analyses have also confirmed considerable overall differences associated with gender and socio-economic groups and these were intertwined with ethnic background. Indeed, when I tried to explain the variation in exam results that existed amongst the young people in this sample, I found that both these former factors were potentially more influential than ethnic differences. This finding does not, of course, diminish the importance of ethnic differences. These still persisted, even when socio-economic group and gender were taken into account. But ethnic background and socio-economic grouping are, of course, closely linked; a person's socio-economic grouping reflects the cumulative influences of their parents' educational and employment related experiences, as well as any difficulties or discrimination that are (or have been) associated with these.

Perhaps the most important point, however, to emerge from this stage of the analysis was how little of the overall variation in examination performance these three background factors jointly 'explained' (just over ten per cent). Building on this observation commentators have recently emphasised the importance of attempts to explain the school experiences of ethnic minority young people and the differential impact of the educational institutions they have attended upon their subsequent academic performance (see e.g. Parekh, 1983, and Smith and Tomlinson, 1989). What is also of note is that examination results achieved at the age of 16 have a crucial importance for the choices made and the opportunities in the period after compulsory schooling ends. This will be seen in the next chapter.

5 Post-compulsory education

Introduction

This chapter has two major parts. The first is about the decision to stay on in education post 16 and young people's reasons for doing so; the second is about how they make use of post-compulsory education once they have decided to stay on.

Much previous research has shown high post-16 participation rates for both Afro-Caribbean and Asian students. Most of this research, however, has been based on surveys in a small number of local authority areas, many of which have been in London. The nationally representative sample here enables us to provide a more general perspective. The decision to stay on at 16 is a particularly important one. Other research carried out using the Youth Cohort Study data shows that, in general, most young people who leave at 16 do so for good; there were relatively few, at the time of the study, who rejoined full-time education at a later stage (Gray and Sime, 1990).

The decision to leave is affected by many factors: differences in the aspirations that young people have, differences in the advice and pressure they receive from various quarters as well as differences in their commitment to education. I shall explore some of these factors and draw on the findings of related studies to contextualise the results.

In the second part of this chapter there are three recurring themes. First, the question of which courses young people take (the issue of participation); second, the achievement of individuals on these courses (attainment); and third, the outcomes which result from this participation in terms of moving to other courses (the issue of transitions).

As far as post 16 participation is concerned I have been able to explore more fully than some other studies the types of courses which young people pursue in post-compulsory education. Taking A levels is still the single most common course of study, but it now only accounts for about one half of all students. Vocational qualifications are also important but there has been little research about differences between ethnic minority and white young people in this respect, mainly because there have been few recent studies which have included further education colleges (see Eggleston et al, 1986). There is also some evidence of ethnic minority young people staying on to retake O levels to improve their fifth year qualifications; this is particularly the case amongst Asians. This latter issue needs further exploration, especially the question of the benefits to be gained from such a course of action.

As far as attainment is concerned, I have already shown that young people begin this post-compulsory period from different starting points in terms of attainment. A particular question which this chapter addresses is how young people build on these achievements in the post-compulsory years. Recent studies of the achievements of ethnic minority children in secondary schools have shown that their progress between the ages of 11 and 16 is similar to that of white children, given their attainment at 11 (Smith and Tomlinson, 1989). A similar question needs to be considered for the 16-19 year age group. Given their attainments at 16, do ethnic minority and white students make similar progress?

A further issue I hope to address more clearly than in previous studies, mainly because I have more detailed data, is the way in which attainments at 16 structure the choices young people make in relation to post-compulsory education. Are ethnic minority young people any different from white young people in their choices regarding courses, or are the opportunities and constraints fairly similar?

Some of the courses young people take are best regarded as building blocks involving transitions from one stage to the next. These transitions may be between courses (for example, between retaking O levels and taking A level courses) or they may be transitions into the labour market or into higher education. Do ethnic minority young people tend to make similar transitions to white young people or are there differences here?

Table 5.1: Participation rates in full-time education by ethnic origin and gender

	PC1	PC2	PC3		
			Excluding higher education	Higher education	No. of cases (sweep 1)
	(%)	(%)	(%)	(%)	
Afro-Caribbean					
Male	45	31	14	7	227
Female	57	45	20	3	256
All	51	39	18	5	483
Asian					
Male	68	63	41	14	526
Female	65	56	38	8	384
All	67	59	40	11	910
White					
Male	32	25	9	7	13,134
Female	42	32	9	6	12,949
All	37	28	9	7	26,082

None of these

Male	31	23	15	4	471
Female	38	27	10	5	514
All	35	25	12	5	985
All	38	29	10	7	28,460

Base: All respondents

The decision to stay on

There is a strong tendency for ethnic minority young people to stay on at school or college. I am particularly concerned in this chapter with full-time post-compulsory education. Table 5.1 gives the participation rates for different groups. Initially, for the year following CSE and O level examinations, four out of ten white young people stayed on, whilst five out of ten Afro-Caribbeans and nearly seven out of ten Asians did so. Two years later the number of white young people in post-compulsory education had fallen to 9 per cent. For the Afro-Caribbean and particularly the Asian groups, however, the numbers remained high. Amongst Asians 40 per cent were still in the education system. If higher education participation is added to this the numbers of Asians in education exceeded 50 per cent; in other words this was an activity of the majority, not the minority (see Figure 5.1). Higher education only features as a small part of the succeeding analysis, so for the remaining tables participation in higher education is not included, unless explicitly stated.

Gender differences are of importance here because it is generally found that girls are more likely to stay on than boys, at least initially. This is indeed the case for all ethnic groups except the Asian group where girls were slightly less likely to stay on than boys.

These findings clearly reflect the high commitment of ethnic minority young people at this stage to the education system. What are the factors affecting the decision to stay on in general? The decision is a complex one and there are both 'push' and pull' factors (Gordon, 1981). The 'push' factors relate to young people's attainments, aspirations, experiences and expectations of school and further education. This is also related to family pressures and parents' own experiences. The 'pull' factors are about the attractions of work and income (Raffe and Willms, 1989; Micklewright, Pearson and Smith, 1990). Local labour markets and unemployment have a number of effects. If youth unemployment is high, this may tend to discourage early leaving (the 'discouraged worker' effect) but, on the other hand, parental unemployment reduces family income and works in the opposite direction, encouraging early leaving because the family needs a wage earner. The empirical evidence on the balance of these factors is conflicting.

Whether or not these various factors operate in a similar way for ethnic minority young people is a somewhat different question. Previous research has shown that ethnic minority young people have high academic aspirations (Eggleston et al, 1986; Cross, Wrench and

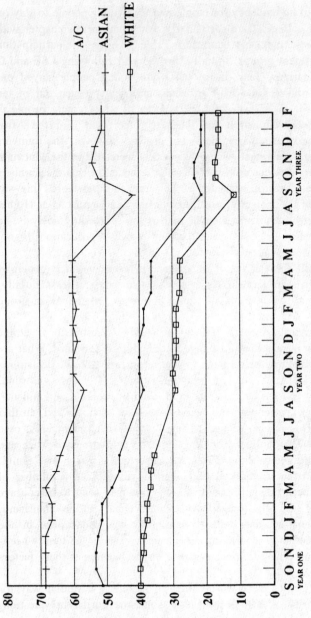

S O N D J F M A M J J A S O N D J F M A M J J A S O N D J F
YEAR ONE   YEAR TWO   YEAR THREE

— A/C
—|— ASIAN
—□— WHITE

Note: Participation from September of the third year includes those moving into Higher Education

Figure 5.1 Percentage in full-time education by ethnic origin

Table 5.2: Attitudes to school by ethnic origin

	Afro-Caribbean (%)	Asian (%)	White (%)	None of these (%)
School has helped to give me confidence to make decisions	52	67	53	51
School has been a waste of time	10	8	11	15
School has done little to prepare me for life when I leave school	54	45	54	53
School has taught me things which would be useful in a job	58	64	55	56
No. of cases	483	910	26,082	985

Base: All respondents

Barnett, 1990). The major factor that is different, however, relates to the likelihood of racism operating in the labour market. In general a somewhat different labour market conditions operate for ethnic minority people; their chances of having a job, their pay and their status are likely to be worse than for white people (Brown, 1984). In 1985, at about the time survey respondents were beginning to consider entry to the labour market, over 30 per cent of Afro-Caribbean men, 28 per cent of Indian men and 37 per cent of Pakistani and Bangladeshi men in the 16-24 age group were unemployed compared with less than 20 per cent of white men (Department of Employment, 1987). Having qualifications seems only partly to have offset this (Clough, Drew and Jones, 1988). The existence of such factors exerts a powerful influence to stay on, despite the financial hardship caused in families with unemployment and the sacrifices involved. It is the distress associated with unemployment and the insecurity of low status jobs that many ethnic minority young people are seeking to avoid in working for qualifications and skilled or non-manual occupations.

The evidence from my study adds weight to these findings. Some of the factors affecting the decision to stay on have already been noted in the previous chapter. A number of these are ones which would lead us to predict early school leaving for ethnic minority young people: the lower average attainment of Afro-Caribbeans, the higher levels of ethnic minority unemployment, the smaller numbers of ethnic minority young professional households or families where parents have a degree, and the tendency to live in the inner city where unemployment is high.

Other factors investigated are ones which are examples of the 'push' factors for staying on. Table 5.2 shows the responses of ethnic minority and white young people to a range of questions reflecting their attitudes to school. Ethnic minority young people, in general, have attitudes which are either as positive or more positive than their white counterparts. They were less likely, for example, to say that school was 'a waste of time' and more likely to say that school 'had taught them things that would be useful in a job'. Since ethnic minority young people fall predominantly into the working class group this feature is particularly noticeable because this latter group often has more negative responses than other groups to school experiences.

Table 5.3 shows the advice about whether or not to stay on in full-time education received by young people. When one considers that 51 per cent of Afro-Caribbeans, 67 per cent of Asians and 37 per cent of whites actually stayed on, the striking feature of this table is the

95

Table 5.3: Source of advice given on whether or not to stay on in full-time education by ethnic origin*

	Advised to stay (%)	Advised to leave (%)	No advice given (%)	Total (%)	No. of cases
Afro-Caribbean					
Careers service	32	13	55	100	225
Careers teacher	33	13	54	100	225
Other teachers	41	11	48	100	225
Family	66	17	17	100	225
Asian					
Careers service	37	13	50	100	405
Careers teacher	43	11	46	100	405
Other teachers	43	6	51	100	405
Family	70	18	12	100	405

White

Careers service	26	13	60	99	11,694
Careers teacher	31	11	58	100	11,694
Other teachers	35	9	56	100	11,694
Family	48	27	25	100	11,694

None of these

Careers service	23	13	64	100	439
Careers teacher	28	13	59	100	439
Other teachers	28	11	61	100	439
Family	50	24	26	100	439

| No. of cases | | | | | 12,763 |

Base: All respondents

Notes:
* Results for cohort two only; a different question was asked in cohort three.

Table 5.4: Source of advice given on whether or not to stay on in full-time education by outcome and ethnic origin (b)

Advice:	Advised to stay		Advised to leave		No advice given		No. of cases
Outcome:	Leave (%)	Stay (%)	Leave (%)	Stay (%)	Leave (%)	Stay (%)	
Afro-Caribbean							
Careers service	26	74(a)	38	62	56	44	166
Careers teacher	36	64	45	55	53	47	166
Other teachers	36	64	35	65	51	49	166
Family	43	57	42	58	50	50	166
Asian							
Careers service	19	81	24	76	25	75	296
Careers teacher	16	84	28	72	22	78	296
Other teachers	14	86	29	72	28	72	296
Family	15	85	36	64	35	65	296
White							
Careers service	32	68	72	28	65	35	9,146
Careers teacher	36	64	78	22	64	36	9,146

							No. of cases
Other teachers	37	63	78	22	65	35	9,146
Family	33	67	80	20	78	22	9,146
None of these							
Careers service	41	59	76	24	67	33	323
Careers teacher	50	50	80	20	64	36	323
Other teachers	46	54	76	24	66	34	323
Family	45	55	81	19	80	20	323

No. of cases 12,763

Base: All respondents

Notes:
(a) This table should be read in the following way; 74 per cent of Afro-Caribbeans who received advice from the Careers Service to stay on actually did so and 26 per cent left.
(b) Results for cohort two only; a different question was asked in cohort three.

strong family encouragement to Afro-Caribbean and Asian young people to follow this course of action, advice which it would appear the majority followed.

This is not exactly the case, however, as Table 5.4 illustrates. Here the advice given to an individual is compared with what they actually did. The table shows the response to advice given from each source. Thus Table 5.3 shows that 70 per cent of Asians were advised by their families to stay on; Table 5.4 shows that 85 per cent of those who were advised to stay on actually did so, an indication of the level of agreement between Asians and their parents on this. In general we found that the majority of those who were advised to stay, from whatever source, took this course of action. Asians and, to a lesser extent, Afro-Caribbeans, however, were likely to stay on, even when given contrary advice.

Modelling the decision to stay on

Given the preceding discussion I wanted to model the decision to stay on. This decision depends on a range of factors which are reflected in the variables chosen. The aim is to achieve a parsimonious model, one which fits reasonably well and describes the differences with a small number of variables.

Those variables selected were; examination attainment, ethnic origin, social class, gender and dummy variables for parental education (according to whether or not either parent was a graduate) and single parent families. Logit models were fitted. (For other similar examples see Clough, Drew and Jones 1988; Micklewright, Pearson and Smith 1990; and for a multi level model Raffe and Willms, 1989).

A reasonable hypothesis is that variables related to low income in the family will operate as 'push' factors to encourage early leaving. This is reflected at least in part in social class, single parent families and being in a family where neither of the parents are graduates, although these factors may also contribute to an individual's expectations and aspirations in other ways as well. Parental education has been found, in other analyses, to have become a factor of significant importance over and above social class (Burnhill, Garner and McPherson, 1990).

I considered the possibility of including other variables. However, apart from a general reluctance to complicate the model unduly, there were other reasons for not adding further variables. Parental income was believed to be a strong 'push' factor but there was no income question in the survey so this could not be included. Parental unemployment was considered as a proxy for low income but, in a separate analysis, was found not to be significant so this was not included either. The other factors which were considered were those that reflected local labour market characteristics and, in particular, local unemployment rates. However, a parallel study produced on Youth Cohort Study data (Jesson, Gray and Sime, 1991) showed that, despite the findings of a 'discouraged worker' effect in Scotland this effect was not in evidence in England and Wales. I therefore decided not to try to incorporate this in the model either.

Logit models are attractive because it is possible to examine ethnic differences after controlling for other variables. The effects for a model predicting the probability of staying on are given in Table 5.5. There are two ways in which the results make it possible to estimate relative effects: the first is by comparing the variability (deviance) explained by each variable, the second is by a comparison of odds ratios. The larger the deviance explained by a variable, the more significant it is in the model.

Odds ratios make it possible to compare each group with a base group; in this case the base group is those with four or more higher grade passes, who are white, with parents in professional occupations, male, with graduate parents, in two parent families. Odds ratios are greater than one if the probability of a group staying on is higher than for the base group; and the ratios are less than one if the probability of staying on is lower than for the base group.

The results show (using the deviances) that once attainment was taken into account, ethnic origin was the single most important variable in determining the chances of staying on (Table 5.5).

The odds ratios show that a number of factors led to a lower probability of staying on. Whatever the level of the individual's attainment, for example, being in the manual social group, having a non-graduate parent and being in a single parent family were associated with lower staying on rates. The odds ratios also show that, other things being equal, the odds of Afro-Caribbeans staying on were three times higher than for whites; and for Asians they were ten times higher than for whites. These are very large effects indeed. It is interesting to note that odds ratios are multiplicative. The combined effects of being Afro-Caribbean (odds ratio 3.23), being in the manual group (odds ratio 0.51) and having a non-graduate parent (odds ratio 0.60) is the product of the three ratios and is approximately one; that

Table 5.5: Staying on in full-time education at 16: a logit model *

	Deviance explained	Degrees of freedom	Estimate	Standard error	Odds ratio
Grand mean			1.94	0.07	-
Attainment	4,540	2			
4+ higher grades			-	-	1.0
1-3 higher grades			-1.59	0.05	0.2
0 higher grades			-2.82	0.05	0.1
Ethnic origin	299	3			
White			-	-	1.0
Afro-Caribbean			1.17	0.16	3.2
Asian			2.35	0.16	10.5
Other			0.18	0.11	1.2
Social class	248	3			
Professional			-	-	1.0
Intermediate			-0.18	0.05	0.8
Manual			-0.67	0.05	0.5

Gender	Male	132	1	-	-	1.0
	Female			0.46	0.04	1.6
Parental education	Graduate	66	1	-	-	1.0
	Non-graduate			-0.51	0.06	0.6
No. of parents	Two parents	7	1	-	-	1.0
	Single parent			-0.16	0.06	0.9

Pseudo R-square	0.95
Deviance for grand mean	5,571 with 226 degrees of freedom
Deviance for model	279 with 216 degrees of freedom

Notes:

* Base groups are those with 4+ higher grade passes, white, parents in professional occupations, male, graduate parents, two-parent families.

103

is the effects operated in opposite directions and effectively cancelled each other out.

Interaction effects were also fitted to the model and these improved the fit of the model to a certain extent. The main interaction of interest was a gender-attainment interaction and this showed that girls in low-attaining groups were more likely to stay on than boys.

Participation in post-compulsory education

From the detailed information available on the courses and qualifications young people pursued I constructed a five fold classification of the major courses they were taking. 'Two or more A levels' was an obvious cut off point for those studying during the post-compulsory years with an eye on entry to some form of higher education. Three other groupings also suggested themselves: 'National Vocational Level 3 Qualifications' (NVQ Level 3) such as BTEC National Certificates; 'National Vocational Level 1 and 2 Qualifications' (NVQ Levels 1, 2); and 'Four or more O levels' (for fuller details see footnotes to Table 5.6).

In an earlier analysis of Youth Cohort Study data it was shown that there was relatively little mixing of academic (i.e. A levels and O levels) and vocational qualifications (see Gray and Pattie, 1988). However it was found that some decisions did need to be made at the margins about which courses the study programmes of particular young people were mainly directed at. There was also a group for whom it was only possible to establish that some 'other course' was pursued which did not fit into any of the above four categories; in these cases individuals were assigned, wherever possible, to the courses which were most likely to represent the major thrust of their education at this stage.

What are the likely factors that affect the participation of ethnic minority young people? Levels of attainment at 16, aspirations and commitment to education were likely to be important factors. Eggleston found that a much larger number of Afro-Caribbean and Asian young people, when compared with whites, gave as their reason for staying on that they wanted to go on to higher education (Eggleston et al, 1986). This factor was particularly strong for Asians and might be expected to affect the kinds of courses they chose to pursue. Also ethnic minority students who had lower fifth year attainments realised it might take them longer than others to achieve this higher education goal; they were, for example, more likely than

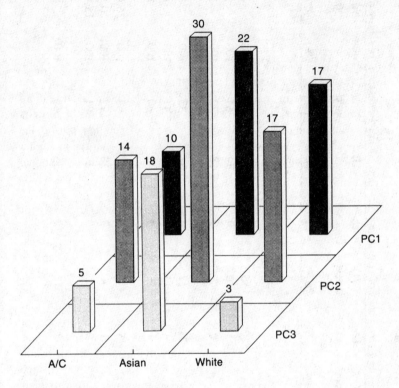

All respondents: combined cohorts

Figure 5.2 Participation in 2+ A levels by year and ethnic origin (percentages)

Table 5.6: Course participation during three years of full-time post-compulsory education by ethnic origin

	2+ A levels (%)	NVQ level 3 (%) (a)	4+ O levels (%)	NVQ levels 1,2 (%)(a)	Other courses (%) (a)	All parti-cipants (%) (b)	Non parti-cipants (%)	Total (%)	No. of cases
Afro-Caribbean									
PC1	10	3	10	16	6	51	49	100	483
PC2	14	5	1	10	4	39	61	100	350
PC3	5	6	0	2	2	18	72	100	243
Asian									
PC1	22	3	21	12	4	67	33	100	910
PC2	30	7	4	11	5	59	41	100	697
PC3	18	11	1	3	4	40	60	100	501
White									
PC1	17	3	5	7	3	37	63	100	26,082
PC2	17	3	1	4	3	28	72	100	20,515
PC3	3	2	0	1	2	9	91	100	15,943
None of these									
PC1	9	1	7	11	3	35	65	100	985

PC2	12	3	1	6	3	25	75	100	715
PC3	5	3	0	1	2	12	88	100	553
All									
PC1	17	3	6	8	3	38	62	100	28,461
PC2	17	3	1	5	3	29	71	100	22,277
PC3	3	2	0	1	2	10	90	100	17,240

Base: All respondents

Notes:

(a) The following courses and qualifications were coded into the 'NVQ level 1,2', 'NVQ level 3' and' 'other courses' categories:

'NVQ level 3' - BTEC National Certicate/Diploma or Higher Certificate in Office Studies or TEC Level 2 or above or ONC/OND or any other National Certificate/Diploma.

'NVQ level 1,2' - Other Vocational Certificates or Diplomas at Level 1 or Level 2 (including BTEC, CGL1, RSA, Pitmans, TEC (Level 1), Technical Studies, CPVE and Regional Examining Bodies Courses).

'Other Courses' - All courses not specified above including one A Level, 1-3 O Levels, etc, courses not clear or not codeable, courses for which no qualifications were aimed for. The categories were mostly mutually exclusive; where courses overlapped the course which came higher on the list was assigned.

(b) This group includes all those on courses shown and also those who gave insufficient or no information about their courses.

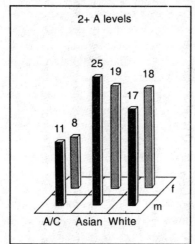

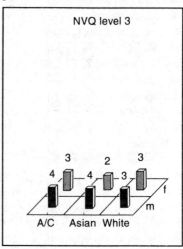

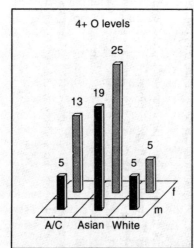

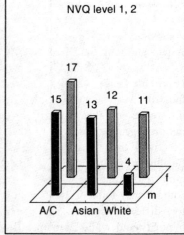

Figure 5.3 Participation in PC1 courses by gender and ethnic origin (percentages of whole cohort)

108

white students to envisage taking A levels in the equivalent of the third year sixth or later. Table 5.6 gives the overall patterns of participation for the whole group. For white students the most popular choice was taking 2 or more A levels over a two year period and then leaving. For Afro-Caribbean students the most likely decision was to take vocational qualifications or O levels in the first year and A levels in the second. For Asians there was a strong emphasis on the 'academic' route of O levels and A levels with particularly large numbers taking O levels in the first year (four times as many as the white cohort) and large numbers taking A levels in the second year (Figure 5.2). A significant number of this Asian group were continuing with study for A levels in the third year.

Attainment is strongly related to the courses young people choose, particularly in the first year (Table 5.7) and whether they stay on (see Figure 5.1). Those with high attainments were more likely to stay on regardless of ethnic origin; the majority of this group took A levels. For those in the middle attainment band taking O levels was the most popular choice, particularly for Asians; this reinforces my earlier comments about Asians pursuing an 'academic' route through further education. High percentages of ethnic minority young people also stayed on in the lowest attainment band; this was mainly for vocational qualifications but there was also a significant group of Asians studying for O levels.

My analysis of participation rates and courses shows that the most important factor which structured choices post 16 was attainment at the fifth year stage. This was true for all ethnic groups; the main difference was that the participation rates were higher for the ethnic minority groups throughout and at almost every level of attainment.

Given this, and the somewhat lower attainments of the Afro-Caribbean group at 16, it seems relevant to ask whether ethnic minority young people were much less qualified than whites for the courses they took? Table 5.8 shows this to be true to a certain extent for different courses. In general the difference between ethnic minority and white participants was equivalent to about one O level pass at grade C.

Gender differences were also explored at this stage. Other research studies have found that Afro-Caribbean males performed less well at 16 than females. In this study, however, such differences were found to be small (see Table 4.3). Girls obtained slightly better results than boys on average at the O level stage. Given this, the pattern of course choice in the first year is interesting (Table 5.9 and Figure 5.3). Afro-

Table 5.7: Course participation during the first year of full-time post-compulsory education by ethnic origin and attainment

	2+ A levels (%)	NVQ level 3 (%)	4+ O levels (%)	NVQ levels 1,2 (%)	Other courses (%)	*All parti-cipants (%)	Non parti-cipants (%)	Total (%)	No. of cases
Afro-Caribbean									
4+ higher grades	68	4	9	4	2	87	13	100	55
1-3 higher grades	7	6	18	13	13	61	39	100	139
0 higher grades	0	2	6	20	3	39	61	100	288
All	10	3	10	16	6	51	49	100	483
Asian									
4+ higher grades	83	5	5	2	1	96	4	100	214
1-3 higher grades	9	4	43	17	4	80	20	100	239
0 higher grades	1	2	18	15	6	47	53	100	457
All	22	3	21	12	4	67	33	100	910
White									
4+ higher grades	61	7	2	3	3	76	24	100	6,830
1-3 higher grades	4	3	13	12	5	40	60	100	6,908

0 higher grades	0	1	3	7	2	14	86	100	12,345
All	17	3	5	7	3	37	63	100	26,082
None of these									
4+ higher grades	64	5	5	4	3	82	18	100	128
1-3 higher grades	3	3	13	19	6	47	53	100	249
0 higher grades	0	0	5	10	2	20	80	100	608
All	9	1	7	11	3	35	65	100	985
All	17	3	6	8	3	38	62	100	28,461

Base: All respondents

Notes:
* This group includes all those on courses shown and also those who gave insufficient or no information about their courses.

111

Caribbean and Asian girls were more likely than their male counterparts to be taking O levels and the reverse was the case for A levels.

At what type of institution did young people study? I created two categories: those who continued their studies in school sixth forms or sixth form colleges (whom we call sixth formers) and those who moved into colleges of further education or tertiary colleges (whom we call FE participants). Afro-Caribbean students were more likely than white students to be FE participants whilst Asians were more likely than white students to be sixth formers, particularly the girls (see Table 5.10).

Eggleston et al (1986) suggested that many young ethnic minoritys tend to use the further education system for both academic and vocational purposes in contrast to whites who use it for predominantly vocational purposes. My findings do not wholly support this. Ethnic minority young people were actually less likely than whites to be taking O levels at college; whilst they were slightly more likely than whites to be taking A levels there, the majority (over 70 per cent) were still staying at school for this (see Table 5.11). The choice of institution of study seems to be largely a function of the particular course(s) which young people want to follow.

The different routes through post-compulsory education serve different purposes. To what extent were these different routes taken by different groups? I consider this question in the next sections looking at each of the major routes (taking O levels, taking A levels and taking vocational courses) in turn.

Improving on O level results

In this section I focus on those young people whose main concern was taking or retaking O levels, their dominant goal being to improve on their O level performance in the fifth year of secondary school. Twice as many Afro-Caribbeans and four times as many Asians compared with whites were taking this route in their first post-compulsory year (see Table 5.6 earlier) and ethnic minority women were more likely to take this route than their ethnic minority male counterparts (see Table 5.9 earlier). This was the largest single difference between Asian and white students in this first year and is the major reason why the participation rate of the Asian group was so much higher overall. What is also readily apparent from Figure 5.4 is that this was only a one year phenomenon. One in five Asians were taking O levels in the

Table 5.8: Mean examination score[a] during the first year of full-time post-compulsory education by ethnic origin and course

	2+ A levels (%)	NVQ level 3 (%)	4+ O levels (%)	NVQ levels 1,2 (%)	Other courses (%)	All participants (%)	Non participants (%)[b]	All (%)	No. of cases
Afro-Caribbean	39	24	22	16	18	23	11	17	450
Asian	42	25	22	17	18	28	9	22	877
White	45	33	25	23	25	35	15	22	25,560
None of these	43	31	22	20	19	28	10	16	961
All	45	33	25	22	24	34	15	22	27,849

Base: All respondents

Notes:
(a) This exam score is based on a scoring system first developed by researchers at ILEA. O levels grades receive the following points: A-7, B-6, C-5, D-4, E-3. CSE grades receive the following points: grade 1-5, grade 2-4, grade 3-3, grade 4-2, grade 5-1. Ungraded results in both exams are scored as zero.
(b) This group includes all those on courses shown and also those who gave insufficient or no information about their courses.

113

Table 5.9: Course participation during the first year of full-time post-compulsory education by ethnic origin and gender

	2+ A levels (%)	NVQ level 3 (%)	4+ O levels (%)	NVQ levels 1,2 (%)	Other courses (%)	All participants (%)*	Non participants (%)	Total (%)	No. of cases
Afro-Caribbean									
Male	11	4	5	15	3	45	55	100	227
Female	8	3	13	17	8	57	43	100	256
All	10	3	10	16	6	51	49	100	483
Asian									
Male	25	4	19	13	4	68	32	100	526
Female	19	2	25	12	5	65	35	100	384
All	22	3	21	12	4	67	33	100	910

114

White									
Male	17	3	5	4	2	32	68	100	13,134
Female	18	3	5	11	4	42	58	100	12,949
All	17	3	5	7	3	37	63	100	26,082
None of these									
Male	8	2	82	8	4	31	69	100	471
Female	10	1	6	15	3	38	62	100	514
All	9	1	7	11	3	35	65	100	985
All	17	3	6	8	3	38	62	100	28,461

Base: All respondents

Notes:

* This group includes all those on courses shown and also those who gave insufficient or no information about their courses.

115

Table 5.10: Institution of study during the first year of full-time post-compulsory education by ethnic origin and gender

	School or sixth form college (%)	College of further education (%)	Total (%)	No. of cases (%)
Afro-Caribbean				
Male	50	50	100	106
Female	49	51	100	148
All	50	50	100	154
Asian				
Male	61	39	100	362
Female	75	25	100	254
All	67	33	100	616
White				
Male	66	34	100	4,545
Female	56	44	100	5,843
All	60	40	100	10,388
None of these				
Male	56	44	100	153
Female	51	49	100	212
All	53	47	100	364
All	60	40	100	11,623

Base: All respondents

first year but less than one in twenty in the second year; most had either moved into the labour market or moved onto other courses.

The fifth year achievements of young people taking the O level route show that this option was appealing to the group of middle attainers (see Table 5.7). This choice could be seen by young people as a reasonable alternative to YTS or direct labour market entry, either as a means of improving their general academic profile to make themselves more attractive to employers, or in order to obtain sufficient qualifications to move on to A levels or other (higher) courses. For Asians this was a frequent choice with 43 per cent in the middle attainment group taking this route. It is worth noting that the take up of YTS was very low for Asians and it is from this middle group that YTS commonly recruits. What is perhaps more surprising is the relatively large number of Asians in the lowest attainment group who stayed on to take O levels whereas for white young people in this group it was quite rare to do so.

116

Table 5.11: Course participation during the first year of full-time post-compulsory education by ethnic origin and institution of study

	2+ A levels (%)	NVQ level 3 (%)	4+ O levels (%)	NVQ levels 1,2 (%)	Other courses (%)	All (%)	No. of cases
Afro-Caribbean							
School	73	18	74	31	33	49	104
FE College	27	82	26	69	67	51	109
Total	100	100	100	100	100	100	213
Asian							
School	80	27	75	51	44	68	392
FE College	20	73	25	49	56	32	183
Total	100	100	100	100	100	100	575
White							
School	88	5	68	31	39	62	5,693
FE College	12	95	32	69	61	38	3,430
Total	100	100	100	100	100	100	9,123
None of these							
School	86	11	74	27	37	55	169
FE College	14	89	26	73	63	45	141
Total	100	100	100	100	100	100	310
No. of cases							10,221

Base: Respondents participating in PC1

117

Table 5.12: Higher grade passes at end of fifth year, at end of PC1 and cumulative number of higher grade passes by end of PC1

| | Number of higher grade passes | | | | | | | | | | | | |
| | at end of fifth year | | | | at end of PC1 | | | | by end of PC1* | | | | No. of cases |
	0 (%)	1-3 (%)	4+ (%)	Total (%)	0 (%)	1-3 (%)	4+ (%)	Total (%)	0 (%)	1-3 (%)	4+ (%)	Total (%)	
Afro-Caribbean	34	51	15	100	28	55	17	100	17	41	42	100	31
Asian	42	52	6	100	40	46	14	100	24	43	32	100	160
White	26	64	10	100	26	57	17	100	12	42	46	100	1,079
None of these	46	49	5	100	39	49	12	100	14	43	44	100	51
All	29	62	9	100	29	56	16	100	14	43	43	100	1,321

Base: Respondents participating in PC1 and taking or retaking 4+ O levels only.

Notes:

* This table should be read in the following way: For those retaking O levels in PC1, 15 per cent of Afro-Caribbeans had 4+ passes at the end of the fifth year, 17 per cent gained 4+ passes during PC1 and, as a result, 42 per cent had obtained 4+ passes in total by the end of PC1.

118

The results at the end of the first year show that many had indeed benefited in terms of improving their profiles (see Table 5.12). Taking four or more 'higher grade' passes as the threshold, about one in ten went into the year with this number of passes and over four in ten came out of the year with this number. The Asian group went into the year less well-qualified than the rest and, not surprisingly, came out the same way although one in three had by now reached the threshold at which taking other courses becomes a more realistic alternative.

One outcome of this extra year was that half the white young people stayed on whilst three out of four ethnic minority young people did so (see Table 5.13). The most popular strategy for all those who stayed on was to move on to taking A levels. There was a small group of Asians with relatively low attainment who were still pursuing 'academic' courses at this stage.

There has been some discussion in the literature (Cross, Wrench and Barnett, 1990) of the way in which careers officers perceive staying on at school to be an Asian phenomenon and, rather than see this in a positive light, regard it as a problem. There was a view that Asians did not realise their own limitations and repeated low level courses with little benefit. Whilst my data might apparently be seen to give some support to this view it needs to be put in some perspective. A considerable number of Asians who stayed on to retake O levels improved their qualifications sufficiently to move on to higher level courses (approximately one half did so) and most did not repeat the year. The total number of Asians with low attainments who continued to pursue 'academic courses' after one year represents only about two per cent of the whole Asian group (table not shown). As Cross, Wrench and Barnett suggest, there is a possibility that stereotypical images lie behind the assumption that there is a problem of 'over aspiration' amongst ethnic minority young people.

Vocational qualifications

Courses which lead to vocational qualifications are diverse in type, in duration and in level. They include such courses as catering studies, office skills, hairdressing, engineering, mechanics, joinery and bricklaying. Some of these are more often pursued on a part time basis, perhaps within a YTS scheme. The courses can be of less than one year in duration or more than two. Equivalences with 'academic' qualifications are at best very approximate. NVQ Level 1 and 2 passes

119

Table 5.13: Course participation during the second year of full-time post-compulsory education for those who took 4+ O levels in PC1 by ethnic origin and attainment by end of PC1

	2+ A levels (%)	NVQ level 3 (%)	4+ O levels (%)	NVQ levels 1,2 (%)	Other courses (%)	All participants (%)(a)	Non participants (%)	Total (%)	No. of cases
Afro-Caribbean									
All (b)	42	12	10	4	7	76	24	100	31
Asian									
4+ higher grades	57	20	0	3	1	87	13	100	51
1-3 higher grades	24	13	12	7	14	73	27	100	69
0 higher grades	13	8	16	23	12	73	27	100	40
All	32	14	9	10	9	77	23	100	160

120

White									
4+ higher grades	32	10	2	6	5	58	42	100	493
1-3 higher grades	7	6	9	8	10	42	58	100	460
0 higher grades	2	1	14	12	9	40	60	100	128
All	18	7	7	8	6	49	51	100	1,081
None of these									
All	27	10	5	10	9	62	38	100	51
All	20	8	7	8	8	53	47	100	1,325

Base: Respondents taking 4 + O levels in PC1.

Notes:
(a) This group includes all those on courses shown and also those who gave insufficient or no information about their courses.
(b) The numbers in this group were too small to breakdown into attainment groups.

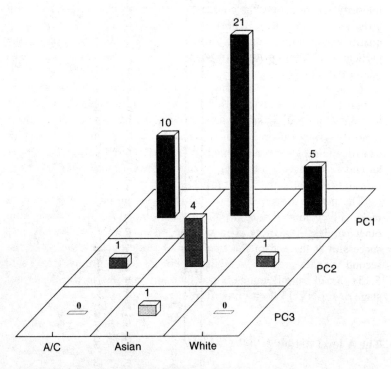

All respondents: combined cohorts

Figure 5.4 Participation in 4+ O levels by year and ethnic origin (percentages)

122

are very roughly of the same standard as O level passes; NVQ Level 3 passes correspond to the sorts of standard that might be obtained by those taking A levels.

In the first post-compulsory year Afro-Caribbean young people were more likely to be studying for vocational qualifications than the other groups and for them it was the most common choice (see Table 5.6). Amongst whites, boys were in a minority, but for ethnic minority young people the courses were as popular with boys as with girls (see Table 5.9). Those who studied for NVQ Level 1,2 qualifications were commonly in the lower attainment bands; the participation rate of Afro-Caribbeans with no higher grade passes was one in five (Table 5.7).

In terms of progression to a second year the findings are very similar to those already reported for O levels (see Table 5.14). About half the white young people stayed on whilst a larger number of ethnic minority young people did so, mainly to continue with similar qualifications. These vocational courses were more likely to be seen as an end in themselves; moving to higher level courses was relatively rare and few continued for a third year.

The diverse nature of these qualifications means it is difficult to make direct comparisons with the results obtained by those taking other routes. It would appear that Asians were somewhat less successful at the end of the first year of study but, at the end of the second year, the results were similar for all ethnic groups (see Table 5.15). Small sample numbers preclude any analysis at the third year stage or for NVQ Level 3 qualifications.

The A level stream

Despite the number of other courses available, taking A levels remains the most common choice amongst those staying on and it remains the most common route into higher education (see Table 5.6). We have seen that some ethnic minority students were not yet in a position to start A level study at this stage and I shall come back to these delayed transitions later. First I shall consider those who followed a conventional pattern and took A levels after two years of study at 18.

It should first be noted that the participation rate for Asians, and for Asian males in particular, was quite high (see Table 5.9) and that in general the fifth year attainments of ethnic minority students taking A levels was somewhat lower than that of whites (see Table 5.8). The participation rate for the Afro-Caribbean group was lower than for

Table 5.14: Course participation during the second year of full-time post-compulsory education for those taking NVQ levels 1,2 courses in PC1 by ethnic origin

	2+ A levels (%)	NVQ level 3 (%)	4+ O levels (%)	NVQ levels 1,2 (%)	Other courses (%)	All participants* (%)	Non participants (%)	Total (%)	No. of cases
Afro-Caribbean	11	5	0	36	13	70	30	100	46
Asian	6	11	5	29	6	61	39	100	93
White	2	4	1	30	6	46	54	100	1,549
None of these	1	10	5	28	3	47	53	100	73
All	2	5	2	30	6	48	52	100	1,761

Base: Respondents taking NVQ levels 1,2 at end of PC1

Notes:
* This group includes all those on courses shown and also those who gave insufficient or no information about their courses.

whites or Asians. For those taking A levels at this juncture I found that Afro-Caribbean students were less successful than their white counterparts although the small number of cases on which this observation is based needs to be noted (see Table 5.16). Around seven out of ten Asians and whites obtain 2 or more A levels by this stage; for Afro-Caribbeans the figure was close to six out of ten.

The question which obviously suggests itself is whether or not these ethnic differences could be attributed to other factors. A multiple regression analysis was carried out using those taking two or more A levels as the group for analysis and the UCCA score as the dependent variable reflecting performance at A level. The independent variables were: the exam score at 16, gender, parental education (whether or not either parent had a degree) and dummy variables for single parent families, social class and ethnic origin. The first three of these variables were statistically significant and together accounted for 35 per cent of the variance. Ethnic origin was not a significant variable. Although this analysis was based on a fairly small number of ethnic minority students, the results suggest that the progress made by different ethnic groups between the O level and A level stages is similar and the weaker results for some ethnic minority students are simply a function of their weaker performance at O level.

The second set of individuals which need to be considered are those who have been retaking O levels in the first year and who, having built on their O level performance, make the transition to A level courses in the second year. We note from Table 5.6 that more Afro-Caribbean and Asian students were taking A levels in the second

Table 5.15: NVQ levels 1,2 passes at the end of PC1 and PC2 by ethnic origin

| | Percentage with one or more passes at end of: | | No. of cases | |
	PC1 (%)	PC2 (%)	PC1	PC2
Afro-Caribbean	61	81	46	28
Asian	44	79	93	50
White	65	78	1,549	710
None of these	56	68	73	33
All	64	78	1,761	821

Base: Respondents taking NVQ levels 1,2 courses at end of PC1 or PC2

Table 5.16: A level passes at the end of the second year of full-time post-compulsory education by ethnic origin and gender

	Mean UCCA score (a)	Number of A level passes				Total (%)	No. of cases
		0 (%)	1 (%)	2 (%)	3+ (%)		
Afro-Caribbean							
Male	5.2	*	*	*	*	100	10
Female	5.1	*	*	*	*	100	10
All	5.1	28	15	11	46	100	19
Asian							
Male	6.3	21	7	20	52	100	75
Female	4.7	33	12	18	37	100	44
All	5.7	25	9	19	47	100	118
White							
Male	6.8	17	12	18	53	100	1,242
Female	6.0	18	13	22	47	100	1,304
All	6.4	17	13	20	50	100	2,547

None of these

Male	5.3	36	17	7	40	100	·23
Female	6.1	6	22	23	49	100	31
All	5.7	19	20	16	45	100	54
All	6.4	18	13	20	49	100	2,738

Base: Respondents who completed the first two years of full-time post-compulsory education and were taking 2+ A Levels.

Notes:

The symbol * denotes numbers too small for calculation of percentages

(a) The UCCA scores were calculated as follows: a grade A at A level was scored as 5, a grade B as 4, a grade C as 3, a grade D as 2 and a grade E as 1.

Table 5.17: The examination results at the end of the fifth year and in PC1 and PC2 for whole cohort compared by ethnic origin and gender

		Percentage of whole cohort with 4+ Higher grade passes at			1+ NVQ passes at 18 (%)	No. of cases
		16 (%)	17 (%)	18 (%)		
Afro-Caribbean	Male	11	12	15	37	108
	Female	12	19	20	32	134
	All	11	15	18	34	243
Asian	Male	25	38	42	25	276
	Female	22	35	35	29	226
	All	24	37	39	27	501
White	Male	25	30	30	25	7,835
	Female	28	32	33	31	8,108
	All	26	31	31	28	15,943
None of these	Male	12	19	19	21	247
	Female	14	18	18	23	306
	All	13	18	19	22	553
All		25	30	30	28	17,240

128

Table 5.18: Examination results and higher education entry at end of PC2 for whole cohort by ethnic origin and gender

| | Percentage of whole cohort | | | |
	With 1+ NVQ 3 passes (%)	With 2+ A level passes (%)	Entering higher education (%)	No. of cases
Afro-Caribbean				
Male	7	6	7	108
Female	4	4	3	134
All	5	5	5	243
Asian				
Male	6	21	14	276
Female	2	13	8	226
All	4	17	11	501
White				
Male	4	12	7	7,835
Female	3	12	6	8,108
All	3	12	7	15,943
None of these				
Male	4	4	4	247
Female	1	7	5	306
All	2	6	5	553
All	3	12	7	17,240

Base: All respondents replying to all three sweeps.

129

year compared with the first, so this group is a significant one. We also find that nearly one in five of the whole Asian cohort was taking

A levels in the third year (Figure 5.2). The outcomes of this in terms of results for these groups are not known because our survey does not reach the end of the third year but these groups will undoubtedly contribute in the long run to some overall improvement in the academic profile of ethnic minority students as a whole.

Overall outcomes

It is now necessary to draw back from a detailed study of the courses followed and consider the cohort as a whole, remembering the high participation rate of the ethnic minority group. The overall effect of this persistence within the education system is striking. Nearly four in ten Asians at 18 now had 4 or more 'higher grade' passes compared with just over three in ten whites (see Table 5.17). Asians were also more likely to have passed 2 or more A levels than any other group (see Table 5.18). Asian males were particularly successful. Afro-Caribbean groups are better qualified, particularly males, in terms of vocational qualifications than any other group. What consequences this has in terms of labour market success has yet to be seen. In terms of immediate entry to higher education, however, it means that Asian participation was particularly high but not Afro-Caribbean participation. (see Table 5.18).

Comparison of these results with those of previous studies shows somewhat better results for ethnic minority students, particularly Asians, than previously estimated (Maughan and Rutter, 1986; Department of Education and Science, 1985). In the DES study, for example, approximately equal proportions of Asian and white school leavers were estimated to have some A levels. My updated findings suggest that more Asians had passed A levels compared with whites at the end of the second post-compulsory year and that this gap was likely to widen as a result of Asians taking further A levels at a later stage.

Summary

In this chapter we have seen that the participation of ethnic minority young people in post-compulsory education is high. The decision to stay on was taken with strong parental backing and the staying on period was used in a variety of ways.

The route that was taken was determined to a large extent by educational attainment at 16, but there are important ethnic differences. It was found for example that a high percentage of Asians stay on to take A levels and also a large group stay on to take O levels and then move on to A level courses. For any ethnic group it is the diversity of participation that is striking though and generalisations about differences need to be made with care.

6 The youth labour market

Introduction

Much has changed in the youth labour market during the last decade.
It bears little resemblance to the labour market of the seventies.
Taking the eighties as a whole, there was a symmetry about the
decade, the recession in the first five years giving way to a partial
recovery in the economy in the last five. Whereas a concern to
mitigate the detrimental effects of youth unemployment dominated the
early part of the decade the later years saw a heightened determination
to enhance skill levels and training amongst young people.

As far as ethnic minority young people are concerned the major
issue has, in the past, been racial discrimination in the labour market.
This was clearly shown in major studies in the sixties (Daniel, 1968),
the seventies (Smith, 1974; and Smith, 1981), and in the eighties
(Brown, 1984). Whilst young people in general are affected by rising
unemployment, ethnic minority young people are sometimes doubly
affected; the unemployment rates for ethnic minorities rise at a faster
rate than for white people in a labour market which is conscious of an
individual's 'race' as well as their qualifications (Field, 1981). In the
latter part of the eighties these problems may have receded somewhat,
as unemployment fell, but much of the evidence for this remains
speculative.

What is true of the labour market in general may also be true of
training in particular. Several authors have argued that inequalities in
the labour market were reproduced in the Youth Training Scheme
(Cross and Smith, 1987; Cross, Wrench and Barnett, 1990) and that
there were further differences in the experiences of ethnic groups with
regard to scheme types and outcomes after YTS.

132

Although ethnic minority young people may have particular concerns they also have similar choices to make and face similar problems to those of white young people. The overall changes that have taken place mean that routes into the labour market have become more complex. It is not simply a case of deciding whether to continue in full-time education or not but whether to take up a training scheme place, enter employment directly or pursue some combination of the options available. Linked with this is the changing value of academic and vocational qualifications. There are now more vocational courses available than before, within both the education system and the training system. Can these qualifications be compared and their relative value to the individual assessed?

A further issue is the growth of youth training provision itself. One year schemes have now given way to two year schemes and these, in turn, have now been replaced by more general youth training leading to recognised national vocational qualifications. Unlike the 'dual' system in Germany, vocational training in Britain has been subject to very rapid change; in some ways it is less rigid than its German counterpart but presents its participants with a more difficult set of choices (Brown and Behrens, 1990).

The picture this presents is a dynamic one. Underlying these rapidly changing circumstances there are other factors which have, for a long time, been known to affect employment opportunities. These include the characteristics of the individual. Apart from ethnic origin, gender and social class may be important. Where an individual lives also matters. The youth labour market cannot simply be considered from the supply side, that is the characteristics of those seeking work; it has a demand side as well. Local labour markets differ and this affects the demand for labour and the availability of training opportunities.

There are a number of difficulties in sorting out what is happening. The most obvious of these is the extent to which, when considering the labour market positions of 16 to 19 year olds, the outcomes are still somewhat uncertain. The final destinations of those remaining in the education and training system remain unknown.

The picture here is therefore an incomplete one. Its strength, as with that of post 16 educational participation, lies in its nationally representative sample; again non response to the later stages of the survey, especially amongst Afro-Caribbean males, may present an overly optimistic picture.

Logit models have been used in a number of places. Their strength is that they go beyond comparison of pairs of variables and enable us to investigate the effects of a number of factors taken together. Logit models also enable us to focus on discrimination. Discrimination, by its covert nature, is difficult to assess in quantitative studies but analyses which control for a whole series of other variables and then still find ethnic differences strongly suggests that such differences result from discrimination.

The major routes

The overall aim of this chapter is to identify the routes that young people take into the labour market. These are not, however, adequately described by the labour market statuses of individuals at particular points in time. What is needed is a more dynamic picture of the various pathways into employment which may involve a combination of different activities.

Evans and Heinz (1990) have noted that 'skills, interests and life plans result from an interplay of personal experiences and institutional requirements'. The transition process is a mix of education, training and employment in varying amounts for each individual. In an earlier analysis of the Youth Cohort Study data, Sime, Pattie and Gray (1990) identified twelve major transition routes. In the present case I have collapsed these into just five (see Figure 6.1).

In the first place we have those who follow an academic route, taking two or more A levels. This is the group most likely to continue with academic study into higher education. It accounted for 16% of the total of all routes taken by young people. Second, we have those in other forms of full-time education (21% of the total). The third group was the largest one, those who use YTS to gain labour market entry (32% of the total). The fourth group is one which has diminished in size during the last decade, namely those who went directly into jobs on leaving school at 16, the 'traditional' leavers (18% of the total). The final group is a residual one and included a sizeable number of people for whom some form of unemployment had been a short or long term experience (12% of the total).

This typology of routes cuts across a static view of labour market activities at one point in time. For example, one in three young people in fact spent some time on a YTS scheme. Although for the majority this may have been immediately after leaving school at 16 this was not necessarily the case: a period of unemployment or full-time education may have preceded the take up of a YTS place. YTS schemes also differed in the range of experiences they offered an individual,

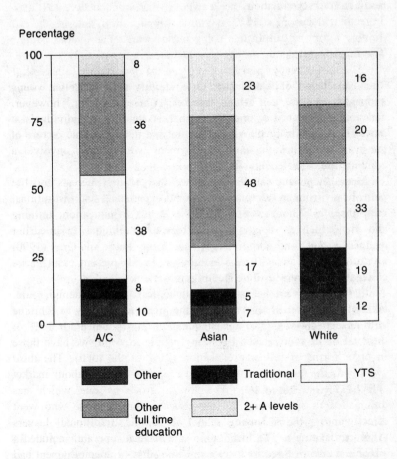

Figure 6.1 Routes into the labour market by ethnic origin (percentages)

although we have mostly chosen to keep them undifferentiated in our analysis for the purposes of presentation.

These route descriptions provide a useful typology of what happened to members of our sample by the age of 19. Initially, however, we need to consider the month by month labour market activities of the sample as a whole. Individuals have to make immediate decisions at 16 by staying on in education, entering YTS or finding a job, or failing this being out of work. The overall patterns for the different ethnic groups are illustrated in Figure 6.2.

As I have already shown, when given the opportunity to leave full-time education the majority took the first opportunity to do so; overall only just over four out of ten stayed on at the age of 16. This figure was rising in the late eighties. Nevertheless, the lower staying on rates post 16 are probably the single feature that distinguishes our system most markedly from others in Europe.

For the respondents in this study their position had shifted considerably but the outcomes differed for each ethnic group. Over six out of ten whites were in jobs, over five in ten Afro-Caribbeans but only three in ten Asians (see Figure 6.3). This picture was, in part, due to the high and continuing involvement of ethnic minority young people in full-time education. However, if those in education are excluded, there are still marked differences; almost eight out of ten (78%) whites were in jobs at this point compared with seven out of ten (71%) Afro-Caribbeans and six out of ten (61%) Asians (see Table 6.12). To the extent that full-time employment was the goal, these differences represented at best incomplete transitions into the labour market and provide cause for concern.

The labour market at 16

Those entering the labour market at 16 face the decision about whether or not to take up a YTS place. One half of all leavers took up a YTS place and one in three took up a job immediately (see Table 6.1). In the analysis carried out here I did not distinguish between jobs in terms of their quality and, in particular, whether they offered training. Among ethnic minority young people it is the small numbers directly entering employment that are particularly of note at this stage. The take up of YTS places by the Afro-Caribbean and white group was fairly similar but for Asians was much lower (see Table 6.2). Only about one in ten of the Asian cohort took up a YTS place and this was the case for both Asian boys and Asian girls. Asian girls were more

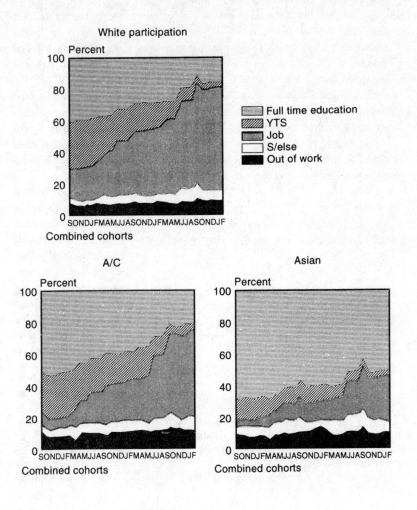

Figure 6.2 Labour market activities 16-19 (cumulative percentages)

137

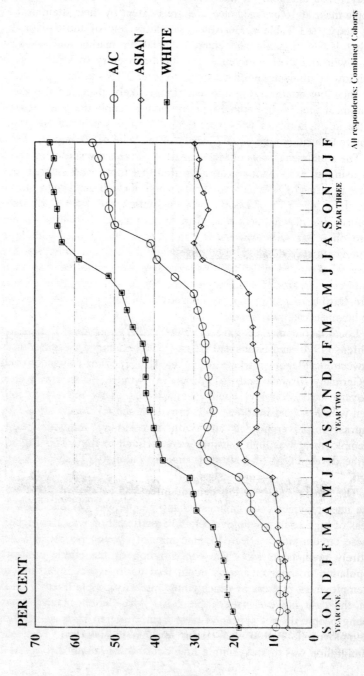

Figure 6.3 Numbers in employment by ethnic origin (percentages)

All respondents: Combined Cohorts

138

likely to be unemployed than Asian boys. The choices that young people make at 16 are mediated to a great extent by their attainment at this stage (see Table 6.3). Amongst whites few of those with the higher levels of attainment entered the labour market and amongst those who did their preference was for direct entry to a job. Those with low attainment were most likely to enter YTS and unemployment for this low attainment group was more likely than for the other attainment groups. For ethnic minority young people the point of note is the small numbers who were entering employment at this stage relative to white young people, whatever the level of attainment.

The attainment levels of labour market entrants are shown in Table 6.4 using an examination score. We find that those who entered jobs were, in terms of O level attainments, about as well qualified as those who took up YTS. I found previously that the Afro-Caribbeans performed somewhat less well than the whites at 16 whilst Asians were on a par with whites. We also know that Asians with high attainments stayed on in very large numbers so, not unexpectedly, those who entered full-time jobs were less well qualified than their white counterparts. The same was true but to a lesser extent for the Afro-Caribbean group; the gap between them and whites for those in the labour market was small.

Local labour markets have an effect at this stage also. Brown and Behrens (1990) and Evans and Heinz (1990) examined the differences between local labour markets in England (Liverpool and Swindon) and in Germany (Bremen and Paderborn). In Swindon, in an area with a buoyant local economy, young people could easily move into jobs even with low qualifications; YTS provision and take-up was low. By contrast in Liverpool, a city with a declining industrial base, unemployment was high and jobs were difficult to find. This had led to the development of a stronger training culture. YTS take up was high.

The general nature of this demand effect can be seen in Table 6.5. The unemployment rate amongst young people was twice as high in areas of high adult unemployment; YTS participation was also higher. These circumstances affected ethnic minority young people in a not entirely predictable way. The concentration of the ethnic minority population in inner city areas might lead us to expect high rates of unemployment in areas in which ethnic minority people lived. This is not the case however (see Table 6.6). Afro-Caribbean and Asian young people do not appear to have been clustered in areas of high unemployment. Part of the reason for this is historical. Post war immigration was to areas with a high demand for labour directly as a

Table 6.1: Labour market activities at 16 by ethnic origin*

	Full-time education (%)	Full-time job (%)	YTS (%)	Out of work (%)	S/Else (%)	Total (%)	No. of cases
All respondents							
Afro-Caribbean	53	7	28	8	5	100	482
Asian	68	5	12	10	5	100	910
White	40	20	31	7	3	100	26,082
None of these	37	19	26	10	8	100	985
All	41	19	30	7	3	100	28,461
Labour market participants only							
Afro-Caribbean	-	15	58	17	11	100	239
Asian	-	15	38	30	17	100	294
White	-	33	51	11	5	100	15,694
None of these	-	31	42	15	12	100	621
All	-	33	50	12	6	100	16,838

Base: All respondents

Notes:

* This and succeeding similar tables are based on replies to the diary question in October in order to establish respondents initial labour market activities. They thus differ slightly from tables in the previous chapter which were based on replies to the diary question in February.

Table 6.2: Labour market activities at 16 by ethnic origin and gender

	Full-time education (%)	Full-time job (%)	YTS (%)	Out of work (%)	S/Else (%)	Total (%)	No. of cases
Males							
Afro-Caribbean	47	9	32	6	7	100	227
Asian	69	6	13	8	4	100	526
White	35	23	33	7	3	100	13,134
None of these	32	20	29	11	7	100	471
Females							
Afro-Caribbean	58	5	24	10	3	100	256
Asian	66	4	11	12	7	100	384
White	45	17	28	6	4	100	12,949
None of these	41	19	23	8	8	100	514
All	41	19	30	7	3	100	28,461

Base: All respondents

141

Table 6.3: Labour market activities at 16 by ethnic origin and attainment

	Full-time education (%)	Full-time job (%)	YTS (%)	Out of work (%)	S/Else (%)	Total (%)	No. of cases
4+ Higher grades							
Afro-Caribbean	88	3	8	2	0	100	55
Asian	97	1	1	1	0	100	214
White	80	11	8	1	0	100	6,830
None of these	83	9	4	1	3	100	128
1-3 Higher grades							
Afro-Caribbean	63	9	21	6	2	100	139
Asian	80	2	10	4	3	100	239
White	44	20	31	3	2	100	6,908
None of these	52	16	25	3	4	100	249
0 Higher grades							
Afro-Caribbean	41	7	35	10	8	100	288
Asian	48	8	19	16	9	100	457
White	16	25	43	12	5	100	12,345
None of these	21	23	31	14	10	100	608
All	41	19	30	7	3	100	28,461

Base: All respondents

Table 6.4: Mean examination score by labour market activity at 16 and ethnic origin

	Full-time education	Full-time job	YTS	Out of work	S/Else	No. of cases
Afro-Caribbean	22	14	11	8	7	483
Asian	27	9	10	8	9	910
White	34	17	15	8	10	26,082
None of these	26	12	11	6	7	985
All	33	16	15	8	9	28,461

Base: All respondents

143

response to labour shortages; for example London Transport recruited in the Caribbean (see Brooks, 1975). As a result, many of the Afro-Caribbean population live in the South-East of England. We should not, therefore, expect a particularly strong association between the size of the ethnic minority population in an area and unemployment for data based (as it is here) on Travel to Work Areas. It should be noted, however, that within such areas it is common to find higher unemployment rates for ethnic minority people compared with white people (Drew and Bussue, 1985) and that the location of ethnic minority people within such areas may be highly clustered.

The Youth Training Scheme

In general, one in three young people participated in YTS and most took up their places immediately on leaving school at 16. Table 6.7 shows the position about three or four months later in the following October. As would be expected the most well qualified were unlikely to follow this route. Some authors have argued that YTS draws largely on the pool of young people who would otherwise be unemployed (Raffe and Willms, 1989). Certainly the advent of two year YTS reduced the number of 17 year olds who were unemployed more than it reduced the size of any other group (Sime and Gray, 1990).

Afro-Caribbean participation in YTS was about as high as that of whites, with higher male than female participation. Asian take up was low. My data set combined two cohorts; the first (beginning 1985) covered the period of one-year YTS and the second (beginning 1986) the period of two year YTS. Whereas the labour market statuses of individuals differed little by cohort at the age of 19, at the age of 17 the differences were marked, with much larger numbers by 1988 on two year YTS (Figure 6.4). Afro-Caribbean participation on YTS amongst 18-19 year olds was higher in the earlier cohort than for whites and this corresponds with the finding that whereas 32% of whites overall followed the YTS route 38% of the Afro-Caribbean group did so.

I used a logit model to study 16 plus participation on YTS for those young people not in full-time education (see Tables 6.8 and 6.9). There are two models. In the first, attainment, ethnic origin, social class, gender and parental education were used as predictors and in the second the local adult unemployment rate was added to take account of local labour market conditions. In the first model only the variables attainment, social class and ethnic origin were statistically

Table 6.5: Labour market activity at 16 by local unemployment rate[a]

Adult unemployment rate[b]	Full-time education (%)	Full-time job (%)	YTS (%)	Out of work (%)	S/Else (%)	Total (%)	No. of cases
High unemployment	40	13	38	8	2	100	2,119
Medium unemployment	45	20	27	6	1	100	3,772
Low unemployment	49	23	22	4	1	100	2,775
All	45	20	28	6	2	100	8,666

Base: All respondents

Notes:

(a) Results for cohort three only, local unemployment rates were only available for this cohort.

(b) The high rate is 16 per cent and above, the medium rate is 10.7 per cent and above and below 16 per cent, the low rate is below 10.7 per cent.

Table 6.6: Local unemployment and ethnic origin*

| | Local adult unemployment rate | | | Total | |
	Low (%)	Medium (%)	High (%)		No. of cases
Afro-Caribbean	26	53	22	100	93
Asian	36	42	23	100	264
White	32	43	25	100	7,878
None of these	37	44	19	100	272
All	32	43	25	100	8,507

Base: All respondents
Notes:
* Results for cohort three only, local unemployment rates were available only for this cohort.

significant. The odds ratios show that participation on YTS was higher, having controlled for attainment, for those in the manual social groups (odds ratio 1.3) and for the Afro-Caribbean group (odds ratio 1.9). Young people from working class or Afro-Caribbean families were more likely to take up YTS, other things being equal.

In the second model, when local adult unemployment rates were added, these differences between ethnic groups and social class groups largely disappeared. The odds of participation in YTS were 2.5 times higher in areas of high unemployment compared with areas of low unemployment. This is an interesting finding and indicates the strong effect that local labour markets had on YTS participation. Areas with a weak labour market and high unemployment had more individuals on YTS than other areas. This finding must, however, be treated with a little caution. The second model was based only on cohort three because local unemployment rates were only available for this cohort. As a result the non-significance of the ethnic differences may be partly due to the sample being reduced by half. It would be reasonable to conclude from the first model that strong ethnic differences exist and from the second model that this effect is mediated by local labour market conditions.

A number of authors (for example, Fenton et al, 1984; and Cross, Wrench and Barnett, 1990) have addressed the issue of equal opportunities within YTS. They have suggested that ethnic minority young people are less likely to be on employer based YTS schemes (mode A schemes in the old classification) than their white

counterparts; these schemes were generally more likely to lead directly
to employment than the non employer based schemes. Differences in
scheme type by ethnic origin cannot currently be investigated with
Youth Cohort Study data. However, I was able to examine variations
in the destinations three months after the end of YTS (see Table 6.10).
I found a lower percentage of Afro-Caribbean and Asian young people
in employment after YTS. Only about five in ten were in full-time
jobs compared with seven in ten white young people. Some caution is
needed in the interpretation of these findings because the sample
sizesfor the ethnic minority groups were small but I found relatively

Table 6.7: Participation in YTS at 16 by ethnic origin, gender and attainment*

	Male (%)	Female (%)	All (%)	No. of cases
Afro-Caribbean				
4+ higher grades	8	8	8	55
1-3 higher grades	26	16	21	139
0 higher grades	39	31	35	288
All	32	24	28	483
Asian				
4+ higher grades	1	0	1	214
1-3 higher grades	10	11	10	239
0 higher grades	21	16	19	457
All	13	11	12	910
White				
4+ higher grades	8	8	8	6,830
1-3 higher grades	34	29	31	6,908
0 higher grades	44	40	43	12,345
All	33	28	31	26,082
None of these				
4+ higher grades	1	6	4	128
1-3 higher grades	23	27	25	249
0 higher grades	36	26	31	608
All	29	23	26	985
All	32	27	30	28,461

Base: All respondents

Notes: See notes to Table 6.1

Table 6.8: Logit model for participation in YTS at 16 for those not in full-time education [a]

	Deviance explained	Degrees of freedom	Estimate	Standard error	Odds ratio [a]
Grand mean			-1.04	0.12	
Attainment[b]	54	2			
4 + higher grades			-	-	1.0
1-3 higher grades			0.87	0.12	2.4
0 higher grades			0.77	0.11	2.2
Ethnic origin	20	3			
White			-	-	1.0
Afro-Caribbean			0.28	0.36	1.3
Asian			0.11	0.36	1.1
Other			-0.82	0.19	0.5
Social class					
Professional					
Intermediate					
Manual					
Gender					
Male					
Female					

Parental education			
Graduate			
Non-graduate			111
Unemployment rate			
Low	-	-	1.0
Medium	0.33	0.08	1.4
High	0.90	0.09	2.5

Pseudo R-square	0.41
Deviance for Grand mean	454 with 178 degrees of freedom
Deviance for Model	270 with 171 degrees of freedom

Notes:

(a) Results for cohort three only; adult unemployment rates were only available for this cohort.

(b) Base group are those with 4+ higher grade passes, white parents in professional occupations, male, graduate parents, living in areas of low unemployment.

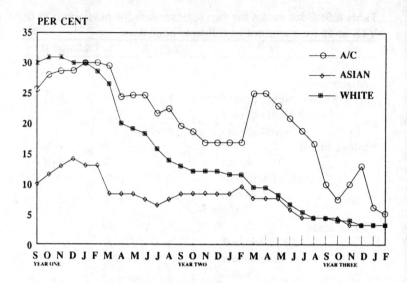

ALL RESPONDENTS: COHORT 2

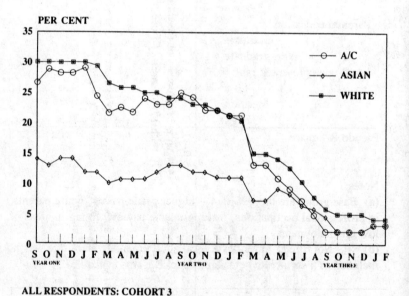

ALL RESPONDENTS: COHORT 3

Figure 6.4 Participation in YTS by ethnic origin (percentages)

150

Table 6.9: Odds ratios for two logit models for participation in YTS at 16 for those not in full-time education

	Model A	Model B
Attainment[a]		
4+ higher grades	1.0	1.0
1-3 higher grades	2.0	2.0
0 higher grades	1.8	2.2
Ethnic origin		
White	1.0	1.0
Afro-Caribbean	1.9	1.3
Asian	0.7	1.1
Other	0.5	0.5
Social class		
Professional	1.0	
Intermediate	1.1	
Manual	1.3	
Gender		
Male		
Female		
Parental education		
Graduate		
Non-graduate		
Local unemployment rate	NF[b]	
Low		1.0
Medium		1.4
High		2.5
Pseudo R-Square	0.34	0.41

Notes:
(a) Base group are those with 4+ higher grade passes, white parents, in professional occupations, male, graduate parents, living in areas of low unemployment.
(b) NF - Not fitted. In Model A local adult unemployment rate was not included as a variable whereas in Model B it was available.

large numbers of ethnic minority young people unemployed. We shall return to this issue later when comparing unemployment in this group with that in other groups.

151

Table 6.10: Labour market activities three months after the end of YTS by ethnic origin

	Full-time education (%)	Full-time job (%)	YTS or government scheme (%)	Out of work (%)	S/Else (%)	Total (%)	No. of cases
Afro-Caribbean	6	48	11	18	18	100	89
Asian	4	51	6	20	20	100	74
White	2	69	5	13	10	100	4,945
None of these	2	61	12	14	12	100	132
All	2	68	6	13	12	100	5,240

Base: Respondents with at least six months participation on a YTS scheme. For those respondents who participated in more than one YTS scheme, the labour market activity three months after the end of the first scheme is shown.

152

Table 6.11: Traditional leavers* in employment at various intervals after leaving school

| | Year one: | | Year two: | | Year three: | | No. of cases |
	October (%)	April (%)	October (%)	April (%)	October (%)	February (%)	
Afro-Caribbean	100	89	89	89	78	87	21
Asian	100	88	88	87	76	86	24
White	100	88	89	86	88	87	3,204
None of these	100	83	82	80	80	82	126
All	100	88	89	86	88	87	3,374

Base: Traditional leavers

Notes:
* Traditional leavers are those who were in employment in October of the first year.

Table 6.12: Labour market activities at 19 by ethnic origin*

	Full-time education	Full-time job	YTS or government scheme	Out of work	S/Else	Total	No. of cases
	(%)	(%)	(%)	(%)	(%)	(%)	
All respondents							
Afro-Caribbean	21	56	4	11	8	100	243
Asian	51	30	2	11	6	100	501
White	16	66	3	9	6	100	15,943
None of these	17	63	3	11	6	100	553
All	17	64	3	9	6	100	17,240
Labour market participants only							
Afro-Caribbean	-	71	5	14	10	100	191
Asian	-	61	5	22	13	100	246
White	-	78	4	11	7	100	13,399
None of these	-	75	4	13	8	100	461
All	-	78	4	11	7	100	14,297

Base: All respondents

Notes:
* This and succeeding similar tables are based on replies to the diary question in February of the third year.

154

Table 6.13: Labour market activities at 19 by ethnic origin and gender

	Full-time education	Full-time job	YTS or government scheme	Out of work	S/Else	Total	No. of cases
	(%)	(%)	(%)	(%)	(%)	(%)	
Male							
Afro-Caribbean	19	65	1	12	2	100	108
Asian	55	27	3	10	5	100	276
White	16	68	4	9	3	100	7,835
None of these	19	62	4	7	8	100	249
Female							
Afro-Caribbean	23	49	6	10	12	100	134
Asian	45	34	2	12	7	100	226
White	16	63	3	10	9	100	8,108
None of these	15	63	3	14	5	100	306
All	17	64	3	9	6	100	17,240

Base: All respondents

Notes:
This and succeeding similar tables are based on replies to the diary question in February of the third year.

155

Traditional leavers

Within the British youth labour market it is still possible for young people to leave school at 16 and find jobs immediately. Such a possibility has practically ceased to exist in other European countries where further education or training are almost the only possible routes. The attainment levels of these 'traditional' leavers (see Table 6.4 earlier) was on average higher than those of any other group, apart from those remaining in education. Their success in the labour market was comparatively good with about 87 per cent still in jobs at the end of the survey (see Table 6.11). There appears to be little difference between ethnic groups in this respect, although the small numbers of cases in the Afro-Caribbean and Asian categories should be noted. I have not, it should perhaps be added, carried out an analysis of wage levels or pay rates nor of the quality of the jobs on offer at this stage. There is no measure, therefore, of job quality. However, the data do indicate that once in employment this group largely continue that way.

The unemployed

Many young people experience short periods of unemployment between the ages of 16 and 19. In considering the sample's experiences of unemployment I was particularly interested in those who had experienced longer periods of being out of work and who were still unemployed by the age of 19. There is also the possibility that not everyone who is out of work is necessarily registered as unemployed, even at the age of 19. I therefore used two definitions to approach these problems. The first group was defined as those who were unemployed at 19, excluding those still in full-time education. The second group was defined as those at the age 19 who were either unemployed or doing something else, excluding those in full-time education. The latter group certainly includes those who are at home with children. However, I believe the number doing this will have been small relative to the number in this group who wished to find (but were unable to) paid employment. Therefore this latter rate possibly reflects more closely the true level of unemployment amongst young people.

It was found that the Afro-Caribbean and Asian unemployment rates were consistently higher than the white rate, whether the first of the two definitions or the second was adopted (see Figure 6.5 andTable 6.12). The differences were more marked when those doing

156

'something else' were included and especially so when confined to labour market participants only.

The percentages of Asian young people out of work at age 19 were particularly marked. It is perhaps a little surprising that the Asian rate is so much higher than the Afro-Caribbean one, especially when compared with statistics from the Labour Force Survey (Department of Employment 1990). There are two possible explanations for this. In the first place it is known that many more Asians than any other group stayed on in education, so those few who wished to find jobs were relatively poorly qualified and therefore more likely to be unemployed. (Table 6.4 provides some support for this argument). In the second place it may be that Afro-Caribbean unemployment is underestimated in the Youth Cohort Study survey due to non response. What I would conclude, in general, is that Asian unemployment was relatively high at 19 and may well have been over 30% , depending on which of the two definitions of unemployment is adopted.

Gender differences in those out of work seem, at this stage, to have been relatively small (see Table 6.13). The correlation between unemployment and cumulative attainment by contrast was very strong (see Table 6.14). Those with A levels were very unlikely to be unemployed whilst those with no qualifications were experiencing unemployment rates of around 16% if they were white and around 25% if they were ethnic minority, even on the more conservative of the two estimates. The effect of local labour markets was also clear. The unemployment rate of young people in areas of high adult unemployment was three times the rate in low adult unemployment areas (table not shown).

Whilst there is an obvious correlation between the route taken prior to age 19 and attainment (only those taking the 2 A level route can have obtained 2 A levels for example) the routes allow us to single out groups who were vulnerable to unemployment and those who seem to have avoided it. The group sizes were small in some cases so the results do need to be interpreted with caution. Those following the A level route had relatively low unemployment rates but so too did those who left school at the first opportunity to obtain jobs, the 'traditional' leavers (see Table 6.15). The particularly vulnerable group was the residual 'other' group which was experiencing relatively high unemployment. So too were those who followed the YTS route,

Table 6.14: Labour market activites at 19 by ethnic origin and cumulative attainment

	Full-time education	Full-time job	YTS or government scheme	Out of work	S/Else	Total	No. of cases
	(%)	(%)	(%)	(%)	(%)	(%)	
Afro-Caribbean							
2+ A levels*	66	34	0	0	0	100	25
NVQ levels 1,2	12	70	2	5	11	100	82
4+ higher grades	46	28	0	19	7	100	26
1-3 higher grades	27	51	12	3	7	100	38
0 higher grades	6	60	3	24	7	100	72
Asian							
2+ A levels	77	19	0	2	3	100	107
NVQ levels 1,2	45	39	1	10	5	100	130
4+ higher grades	84	12	0	3	2	100	110
1-3 higher grades	50	27	2	15	7	100	50
0 higher grades	5	48	9	24	14	100	104
White							
2+ A levels	58	36	0	3	3	100	2,356
NVQ levels 1,2	8	78	3	6	4	100	4,476
4+ higher grades	31	59	1	5	4	100	2,197

1-3 higher grades	8	75	4	8	6	100	1,837
0 higher grades	1	68	6	16	10	100	5,078
None of these							
2+ A levels	64	29	0	4	3	100	45
NVQ levels 1,2	17	69	5	3	7	100	132
4+ higher grades	60	37	0	2	1	100	53
1-3 higher grades	11	72	6	5	5	100	55
0 higher grades	2	68	3	19	8	100	268
All	17	64	3	9	6	100	17,240

Base: All respondents

Notes:

* The 2+ A levels group includes those with NVQ level 3 passes. The NVQ levels 1,2 group comprises those with NVQ level 1,2 passes, whether or not they also have higher grade passes at GCE or equivalent level.

159

Table 6.15: Labour market activites at 19 by ethnic origin and major route

Route taken	Full-time education (%)	Full-time job (%)	YTS or government scheme (%)	Out of work (%)	S/Else (%)	Total (%)	No. of cases
2 + A levels							
Afro-Caribbean	70	30	0	0	0	100	19
Asian	81	13	1	3	2	100	118
White	61	30	0	4	4	100	2,547
None of these	77	20	0	1	3	100	54
Other FTE							
Afro-Caribbean	37	47	1	9	6	100	88
Asian	65	22	0	8	5	100	239
White	26	63	1	6	5	100	3,217
None of these	37	52	1	6	3	100	129
YTS							
Afro-Caribbean	7	62	9	16	7	100	92
Asian	1	54	11	24	10	100	83
White	2	72	9	11	6	100	5,230
None of these	1	69	11	12	8	100	140

Traditional							
Afro-Caribbean	0	93	5	2	0	100	19
Asian	0	86	0	0	15	100	24
White	1	89	1	6	4	100	3,021
None of these	1	85	1	12	2	100	120
Other							
Afro-Caribbean	0	55	0	18	27	100	24
Asian	5	51	2	27	16	100	38
White	1	63	1	20	13	100	1,929
None of these	0	64	1	20	15	100	110
All	17	64	3	9	6	100	17,240

Base: All respondents

Notes:

* The groups are defined as follows; 2+ A levels, respondents taking two or more A levels in PC1 and PC2/Other FTE, respondents participating in full time education either in PC1 or PC2/YTS, respondents participating in YTS for 6 months or more/Traditional, respondents in full time jobs in October of the fifth year/Other, all those not in the above groups. The groups are mutually exclusive. It is possible for a respondent to follow YTS <u>and</u> be in full-time education at some time. Such respondents were placed in the YTS group.

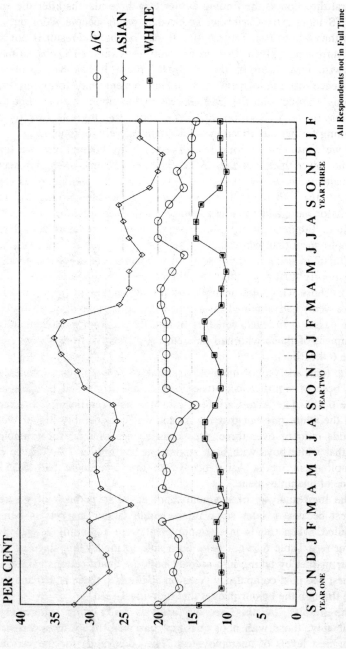

PER CENT

A/C

ASIAN

WHITE

S O N D J F M A M J J A S O N D J F M A M J J A S O N D J F

YEAR ONE | YEAR TWO | YEAR THREE

All Respondents not in Full Time
Education: Combined Cohorts

Figure 6.5 Numbers out of employment by ethnic origin (percentages)

162

particularly Asians and Afro-Caribbeans. This finding is in the same general direction as the finding earlier that three months after the end of YTS more Afro-Caribbean and Asian young people were out of work than whites (see Table 6.10). It may be that the result is not all that surprising, given that many who took up YTS places may otherwise have been in this residual group; it has had a mixed experience of employment and unemployment and forms in our analysis a group with the least success in the labour market. But the progress of the YTS group, relative to those entering jobs directly or obtaining further qualifications, was comparatively disappointing.

If we consider how long young people were unemployed we find that no fewer than four out of ten experienced some unemployment; the majority, however, were only unemployed for short periods (see Table 6.16). About 15% of the group were unemployed for six months or more and some reported unemployment of over two years' duration. Ethnic minority young people experienced more long term unemployment than whites.

Whilst, in general, those who were unemployed for long periods were poorly qualified, this was not necessarily the case (see Table 6.17). Those who were unemployed for six months at least (but less than a year) had obtained on average the equivalent of three higher grade passes at O level, which is little different from the examination attainment of those who had entered a job directly from school (see Table 6.4 earlier).

The logit analysis of unemployment at 16 shows three variables to have been of significance: attainment, ethnic origin and gender (see Table 6.18). The Afro-Caribbean rate was not significantly different from the white rate but that for Asians was considerably higher with an odds ratio of over three. One consequence of this, for example, was that white boys with high attainment had only a 7% chance of unemployment whilst Asian boys with low attainment had a 35% chance of unemployment.

The logit analysis of unemployment at 19 is perhaps of greater interest because a later stage in the youth labour markets is being modelled, when trends in unemployment were beginning to become clearer (see Table 6.19). I have been able to model this stage of the labour market by taking into account both the qualifications gained in the first two post-compulsory years (in addition to those at 16) and the route through the labour market that individual used.

The results of this second analysis are rather interesting. Predictably, those with poor qualifications were likely to experience the highest levels of unemployment. The odds ratios for the various routes show that, for individuals with the same level of qualifications, the 'traditional' route was likely to lead to the lowest levels of unemployment (odds ratio of 0.2), YTS to higher levels of unemployment (odds ratio 0.4) and the residual category of others to a higher level of unemployment still (odds ratio 0.7). Gender, social class and ethnic differences were also significant.

Odds ratios are multiplicative and it is found that being Afro-Caribbean, female and in the manual social group increased the odds of unemployment by a factor of 4.3. Let us take, for example, an individual who took the YTS route into the labour market with three higher grade passes and who had non-graduate parents. If that person was white, male and from a professional background the chance of being unemployed was just 8 per cent. If we take a person who was Afro-Caribbean, female and from a manual social background but was otherwise similar to the white person, the chance of being unemployed was 27 per cent.

The goal of these analyses is to estimate the net effects of direct and indirect discrimination in the youth labour market; these models represent an important step in this direction. The model has its limitations however. There are factors apart from the route into the labour market and qualifications which affect employment chances at the individual level; the number of applications for jobs and methods of job seeking are just two examples. These have not been included. It has been found in other research, however, that ethnic minority young people are just as strenuous in their job searches as other individuals if not more so (see Clough and Drew, 1985). Consequently these factors would probably not account for the ethnic differences found. It could be argued that qualifications should be further disaggregated to reflect differences between individuals but when I did this, in a separate analysis, it made little difference in terms of explaining more deviance or affecting ethnic differences.

Lee and Smith (1989) used a multi level model to consider gender equity in teachers' salary levels in the U.S. They were particularly concerned to identify differences between salaries which were uniquely associated with gender, that is resulted from sex discrimination. They argued strongly for careful variable selection and chose for their analysis a number of factors to reflect qualifications, training and experience. They specifically excluded other individual characteristics. 'Our choice of variables to include was dictated by considering only those measures which could justifiably (their emphasis) be cause for differentiation in salary. Other demographic measures (e.g. age, 'race', ethnicity, marital status, family size) were

164

purposely not included in this study, although there may be some salary differentiation on those measures'. The focus of the Lee and Smith study was on gender equity so 'sex' was the only demographic factor included. If we accept their argument then, by the same token, ethnic origin should be included in our analysis but not social class, gender and parental education. It was our decision to include these other variables because we were interested in how they operated together but it is undoubtedly the case that, had we excluded them, the ethnic effects reported would have been larger than they are shown to be in our tables.

The labour market at 19

We shall now turn our attention to the final labour market destinations of the respondents. Employment and unemployment were, to a certain extent, two sides of the same coin at this stage. In general, few young people were on training schemes and relatively few young people were still in full-time education. For ethnic minority young people this was not, however, the case; the numbers continuing in full-time education were still relatively large as we have already seen.

There are positive and negative aspects to this. Ethnic minority young people were using the education system but at the same time relatively few had secured a place in the labour market (see Table 6.12); only 30%   of Asians and 56% of Afro-Caribbeans. The qualifications that had been gained at 16 or in the succeeding years were of evident importance (Table 6.14). Those with A levels were likely to still be in the education system and white young people with vocational qualifications were the ones most likely to be in jobs.

The routes young people used were also of importance (see Table 6.15). The traditional route of direct labour market entry at 16 led to the highest probability of employment at this stage (89% for whites) whilst the YTS route had a lower probability (72% for whites). The traditional route did seem to be a relatively safe one. Within all of the groups ethnic minority young people generally had a lower chance of being in a job than their white counterparts (except for those who went directly into the labour market at 16 but the numbers here were rather small).

The logit analysis (see Table 6.20) shows the importance of route and attainment in determining the chances of being in employment (85 per cent of the deviance explained by the model is explained by these

Table 6.16: Duration of unemployment by ethnic origin

	Months unemployed						
	0 (%)	1-5 (%)	6-11 (%)	12-23 (%)	24+ (%)	Total (%)	No. of cases
Afro-Caribbean	59	23	11	5	3	100	243
Asian	60	23	7	7	3	100	501
White	63	23	7	6	1	100	15,943
None of these	54	25	8	9	4	100	553
All	63	23	7	6	2	100	17,240

Base: All respondents

Table 6.17: Mean examination score by number of months unemployed and ethnic origin

	Months unemployed						
	0	1-5	6-11	12-23	24+	All	No. of cases
Afro-Caribbean	19	17	17	7	4	17	243
Asian	27	22	17	15	7	24	501
White	25	24	15	9	6	23	15,943
None of these	21	15	9	6	6	17	553
All	25	24	15	9	6	23	17,240

Base: All respondents

166

two factors). The base group was deliberately chosen to be a group which was likely to be quite successful; those who followed the two A level route, successfully obtained two A level passes and were white males with professional and graduate parents. Most of this group continued into higher education. We should remember, though, that this model is based on those who entered the labour market and for these people the A level route did not appear to be very helpful.

The model shows that the qualifications gained and the route chosen are both crucial to employment chances. The A level route was least likely to lead to employment compared with the other routes for those who chose to enter the labour market. Those who left school at 16 (the traditional leavers) were most likely to be in employment relative to those taking other routes. YTS was more likely to lead to employment than the A level route but less likely than the traditional route. The quality of the jobs was not, of course, taken into account here and it may be that jobs obtained after YTS are higher in quality than those obtained on leaving school at the earliest opportunity. This does not alter the fact that the more qualifications one had the better were the chances of employment as the odds ratios for attainment show.

Once these factors are taken into account ethnic origin, social class and gender still remained of importance. In order to illustrate the implications of this model the probabilities of being in a job as predicted by the model are illustrated in Figure 6.6.

We have taken those individuals who were similar in a number of respects: the route they used, their cumulative attainment and parental education. If we take those who are in the residual 'other' group with no O levels and non graduate parents as an example, this group we already know was one in which the chances of employment were relatively poor. The model tells us that there were considerable differences between gender, social class and ethnic groups as well. For white males with professional parents the percentage in employment was 74%, for Afro-Caribbean males with manual parents it was 55% and for Asian females with manual parents it was 36%. These differences are large.

Finally, I have compared what young people actually did at the age of 19 with what they had predicted they would be doing a year earlier (see Table 6.21). There was considerable agreement between the two but there were two areas where what happened differed from what was predicted. In general young people slightly over predicted their likely participation in education and employment and under predicted their chances of being unemployed.

167

Table 6.18: Logit model for unemployment rate[a] at 16[b]

	Deviance explained	Degrees of freedom	Estimate	Standard error	Odds ratio
Grand mean			-2.62	0.13	
Attainment[c]	119	2			
4+ higher grades			-	-	1.0
1-3 higher grades			0.00	0.15	1.0
0 higher grades			0.76	0.13	2.1
Ethnic origin	44	3			
White			-	-	1.0
Afro-Caribbean			0.25	0.28	1.3
Asian			1.24	0.28	3.4
Others			0.75	0.14	2.1
Social class					
Professional					
Intermediate					
Manual	23	1			
Gender					
Male			-	-	1.0
Female			0.30	0.06	1.4

Parental education

Graduate

Non-graduate

Pseudo R-Square   0.56

Deviance for Grand mean 333 with 95 degrees of freedom

Deviance for model   147 with 87 degrees of freedom

Notes:

(a) The unemployment rate is defined as the numbers unemployed or doing something else as a percentage of those not in full-time education.

(b) Results for cohort three only, unemployment rates were available only for this cohort.

(c) Base group are those with 4+ higher grade passes, white parents in professional occupations, male, graduate parents, living in areas of low unemployment.

169

Table 6.19: Logit model for unemployment rate at 19[a]

	Deviance explained	Degrees of freedom	Estimate	Standard error	Odds ratio
Grand mean[b]			-1.66	0.13	-
Route	368	4			
2+ A levels			-	-	1.0
Other FTE			-0.80	0.12	0.5
YTS			-0.90	0.13	0.4
Traditional			-1.71	0.14	0.2
Others			-0.33	0.13	0.7
Attainment	324	4			
2+ A levels			-	-	1.0
NVQ 1,2			0.15	0.14	1.2
4+ higher grades			0.27	0.13	1.3
1-3 higher grades			0.62	0.15	1.9
0 higher grades			1.25	0.14	3.5
Ethnic origin	20	3			
White			-	-	1.0
Afro-Caribbean			0.41	0.20	1.5
Asian			0.79	0.19	2.2
None of these			-0.06	0.14	0.9

Social class	33	2			
Professional			-	-	1.0
Intermediate			0.20	0.08	1.2
Manual			0.44	0.08	1.6
Gender	122	1			
Male			-	-	1.0
Female			0.57	0.05	1.8
Parental education	32	1			
Graduate			-	-	1.0
Non-graduate			-0.46	0.08	0.6

Pseudo R-Square   0.57

Deviance for Grand mean   1,589 with 507 degrees of freedom

Deviance for Model   688 with 492 degrees of freedom

Notes:

(a) The unemployment rate is defined as the numbers unemployed or doing something else as a percentage of those not in full-time education.

(b) Base group are those following the 2+ A levels route, with 2+ A levels, white, professional parents, male, graduate parents.

Table 6.20: Logit model for percentage employed at 19[a]

	Deviance explained	Degrees of freedom	Estimate	Standard error	Odds ratio
Grand mean[b]			1.58	0.12	
Route	487	4			
2+ A levels			-	-	1.0
Other FTE			0.78	0.12	2.2
YTS			0.39	0.12	1.5
Traditional			1.73	0.13	5.6
Other			0.31	0.13	1.4
Attainment	389	4			
2+ A levels			-	-	1.0
NVQ 1,2			-0.17	0.13	0.8
4+ higher grades			-0.29	0.12	0.7
1-3 higher grades			-0.71	0.14	0.5
0 higher grades			-1.26	0.13	0.3
Ethnic origin	23	3			
White			-	-	1.0
Afro-Caribbean			-0.42	0.19	0.7
Asian			-0.80	0.18	0.4
None of these			0.07	0.18	1.1

172

Social class					
Professional	29	2	-	-	1.0
Intermediate			-0.22	0.07	0.8
Manual			-0.39	0.07	0.7
Gender					
Male	80	1	-	-	1.0
Female			-0.42	0.05	0.7
Parental education					
Graduate	28	1	-	-	1.0
Non-graduate			0.40	0.08	1.5

Pseudo R-Square   0.60
Deviance for Grand mean 1,722 with 501 degrees of freedom
Deviance for Model   694 with 486 degrees of freedom

Notes:
(a) Base group are those following the 2+ A levels route, with 2+ A levels, white, professional parents, male, graduate parents.
(b) The percentage employed is defined as the number of employed as a percentage of those not in full-time education.

173

Table 6.21: Activities respondents thought they would be doing in February of year three when questioned a year earlier compared with what they were actually doing by ethnic origin

	Full-time education (%)	Full-time job (%)	YTS government scheme (%)	Out of work (%)	S/Else (%)	Total (%)	No. of cases
Afro-Caribbean							
Expected activity	27	60	4	3	6	100	329
Actual activity	21	56	4	11	8	100	243
Asian							
Expected activity	55	37	1	3	5	100	648
Actual activity	51	30	2	11	6	100	501
White							
Expected activity	19	73	2	3	4	100	19,456
Actual activity	16	66	3	9	6	100	15,943
None of these							
Expected activity	18	73	1	4	5	100	666
Actual activity	17	63	3	11	6	100	553
All							
Expected activity	20	72	2	3	4	100	21,099
Actual activity	17	64	3	9	6	100	17,240

Base: All respondents

174

Route	Attain	Ethnic Origin	Social Class	Gender	Percentage Employed at 19	
TRAD	1-3	WHITE	PROF	MALE	95	
		A/C	MAN	MALE	90	
		ASIAN	MAN	FEMALE	80	
YTS	1-3	WHITE	PROF	MALE	84	
		A/C	MAN	MALE	70	
		ASIAN	MAN	FEMALE	51	
OTHER	0	WHITE	PROF	MALE	74	
		A/C	MAN	MALE	55	
		ASIAN	MAN	FEMALE	36	

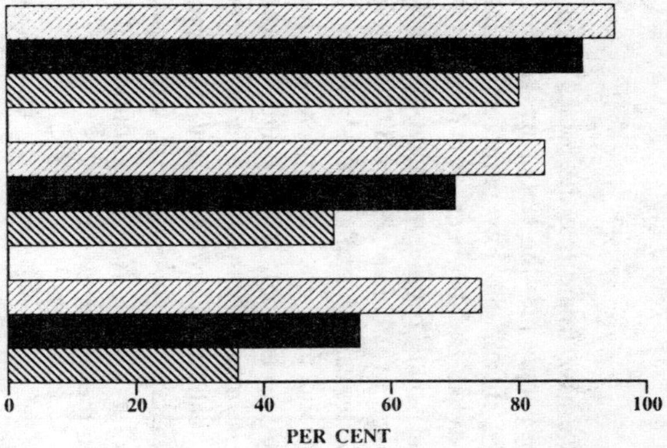

PER CENT

Figure 6.6 Predicted employment probabilities at 19 for selected groups (percentages)

Summary

In this chapter we have found that the routes taken by ethnic minority and white young people into the labour market differ considerably. A good example of this is the low participation rate of Asian young people in YTS. What has also been shown is that Afro-Caribbean and particuarly Asian young people are much less likely to be established in jobs by the age of 19 than their white counterparts. Educational participation alone cannot explain this. When the transitions are modelled it is found that, once attainment and route into the labour market are taken into account, ethnic origin (at least when odds ratios are considered) is invariably the single most important factor. This in all cases means that Afro-Caribbeans and, to a greater extent, Asians are at a disadvantage relative to their white peers. This provides strong indirect evidence for the continuing effects of racial discrimination in the labour market.

7 Conclusions

> Colour is always there. A second-generation Irishman - even a
> second generation Jew - can pass for English. But not a second-
> generation Jamaican. Ethnic minority is always ethnic minority.
> It's always there, the difference.

Quote in Daniel (1968:127)

Although this comment was made 25 years ago it is still very pertinent
today. The questions I want to ask in conclusion are about the extent
to which the findings of this study reflect a continuity in the
experiences of ethnic minority young people compared with those of
the past and the extent to which changes can be detected for better or
worse.

Relative to the experiences of those who arrived in the first wave of
post war immigration in the fifties we might expect to find change.
These early immigrants were unfamiliar with the language and the
culture and experienced widespread discrimination which was not, at
that time, illegal. We might expect that familiarity with Britain and an
improvement in educational qualifications would lead to a general
improvement in the economic position of the children of these
immigrants. By the early eighties studies were, however, showing that
this expected improvement was not taking place. Brown (1984:123)
concluded his PSI report by noting this. 'The early immigrants fitted
into specific localities, parts of the housing stock and corners of the
economy that had been vacated by sections of the white working class
who had moved on to better things. They tended to remain within
these specific sectors because of racial discrimination and because of
the mutual reinforcement of a network of interlocking disadvantages.

The present findings show that the more recent migrants and the children of the earlier migrants are still confined, for the most part, to these same areas and sectors of the economy, while the signs of economic regeneration are elsewhere. For the most part, therefore, Britain's well established ethnic minority population is still occupying the precarious and unattractive position of the earlier immigrants. We have moved, over a period of 18 years, from studying the circumstances of immigrants to studying the ethnic minority population of Britain only to find that we are still looking at the same thing.'

There are other reasons why we might expect to see the fortunes of ethnic minority young people change in the eighties. The period itself was a period of change. Equal opportunity policies were being put in place in education by local education authorities and in YTS and by some employers. It might be hoped that this would improve ethnic minority young people's chances in the labour market. On the other hand significant changes were being made to the structure of industry with the decrease of manufacturing and the increase of the service sector, changes which led to large increases in unemployment. Such changes might advantage some ethnic minority young people but would be likely to disadvantage large numbers of others.

In conclusion I need to summarise the findings about educational performance at 16, about experiences of post-compulsory education and about entry into the labour market and ask whether these experiences reflect a continuity with the past or whether new and significant changes have taken place.

Firstly, though I need to make a summary point about the methodology. This study reflects a sizeable improvement on the past in the way we have studied the transitions of ethnic minority young people between the ages of 16 and 19. The Youth Cohort Study is the first nationally representative survey of its kind and provides a very large sample of white young people against whom we can contrast the experiences of our ethnic minority respondents. This is very important when we consider the detail required to reflect, within a single study, the experiences of different groups of people, those who stay on at school or college, for example, or those who take up YTS places and those with high attainment levels as opposed to those with few or no qualifications at all. Analysis of these groups has enabled us to move beyond simplistic generalisations about Afro-Caribbean and Asian young people for example their supposed underachievement and to chart the diversity that exists between and within the groups.

What I would also suggest is that the methods of analysis used in this study, and in particular the logit modelling procedures, provide a further improvement on the analysis previously carried out in this area. It is by controlling for educational attainment and other relevant variables that we can most clearly see the extent to which the problems of ethnic minority young people persist in the youth labour market.

Home and school at 16

When it comes to the home backgrounds of the respondents the study reflects patterns of economic disadvantage that are well known.

Ethnic minority young people were predominantly from working class homes (over 60 per cent), their parents were up to three times as likely as white parents to be unemployed, and they were also three times as likely to be living in the inner city. In other words the ethnic minority groups suffered from being over represented in the particular social class groupings (the manual group), employment groups (the unemployed) and geographical groups (the inner city) which were most disadvantaged. It should be made clear however, that not all ethnic minority young people were in this situation; there was a significant minority whose parents were in professional jobs and who did not live in the inner city. This group, whilst rather small, is of importance because I would expect its academic attainment and progress to be more akin to the white middle class group than to the ethnic minority working class one.

Educational attainment at 16 reflects both a continuation of past trends and a pattern of change. Whilst the attainment of Asian and white young people at the O level stage at 16 was similar, the attainment of Afro-Caribbean young people, on average, lagged behind. The size of the difference depended on the measure being used. For those obtaining 4 or more higher grade passes the difference was stark, about one in four Asians and whites crossed this high hurdle but only one in ten Afro-Caribbeans. If the average exam score is used, based on the grades of passes both at O level and in CSE examinations, the differences are smaller. Whites and Asians were doing about a third better than Afro-Caribbeans. I also analysed this data by ethnic origin, socio-economic group and gender taken together. Analysis of variance showed that, of these three variables, socio-economic group was the most important, that is, socio-economic group differences were the largest of all. That is not to say that ethnic differences disappeared when socio-economic group was taken into

179

account. Ethnic differences still persisted within socio-economic groups although such differences were usually small. It would be interesting to see future data analysed in this way, because despite the difficulties in defining socio-economic groups appropriately, the interaction of social class with ethnic group is important.

These differences reflect past trends. Previous surveys have shown the Afro-Caribbean group, on average, to be lagging behind. But there is also a pattern of change. The estimate obtained of Afro-Caribbeans obtaining five or more 'higher grade' passes was higher than those of previous studies, so there would seem to be some improvement.

Post-compulsory education

The single most significant finding relating to post-compulsory education was the high participation rate of ethnic minority young people. Whilst 37 per cent of whites stayed on in full-time post-16 education, 51 per cent of the Afro-Caribbean group did so and 67 per cent of the Asian group. By the third post-compulsory year the differences were, if anything, starker still with over 50 per cent of Asians and over 20 of Afro-Caribbeans remaining in some form of further or higher education compared with around 16 per cent of whites. These differences illustrate the high commitment of ethnic minority young people to staying on in education as well as strong family support for continuing. A much higher percentage of ethnic minority parents than white parents were reported to have encouraged their children to stay on.

Statistical modelling of the decision to stay on showed that, once attainment was taken into account, ethnic origin was the single most important factor in determining the chances of staying on; it outweighed all other socio-economic characteristics. The tendency for those in the lower socio-economic groups to leave school at the earliest opportunity was not found to be the case for Afro-Caribbean and, particularly, Asian young people.

The high participation rate of ethnic minority young people reflects the findings of some previous studies. The strength of this study is that I was able to analyse in much greater detail than previous studies the pattern of participation in post-compulsory education and the types of courses which were preferred by young people with different levels of attainment.

Once young people were involved in the post-compulsory education system the picture became a little more complex. In simple terms it

180

can be said that whites were more likely than others to opt for the traditional academic route of taking two or more A levels whilst Afro-Caribbeans were more likely than other groups to be taking vocational courses. Some Asians were adopting a deferred academic route; a high percentage took or retook O levels within the first post-compulsory year and then subsequently moved on to A level courses. There was considerable diversity here, however, and it is important not to over simplify. There was, for example, a group of Afro-Caribbeans who took A level courses and then went on to higher education in the normal way. To a very great extent these choices seem to have been determined by attainment at sixteen. Since we have found that the Afro-Caribbean group lagged behind the others in examination attainment terms at this stage it is not surprising to find that Afro-Caribbean young people were over represented on those vocational courses which tended to recruit from amongst young people with middling levels of qualifications.

Given the high participation rates of ethnic minority young people in post-compulsory education we might expect to find that, compared with their white counterparts, ethnic minority young people were less well qualified in terms of fifth year qualifications to take the courses they did. This was, in fact, the case, although the differences were not particularly large.

Other authors have argued that ethnic minority young people were inclined to use further education colleges for academic and vocational study, in contrast to whites who used such colleges predominantly for vocational study. I did not find this. In my view the choice of institution seemed to be largely a function of the course which an individual wanted to follow; in this sense there was no strong evidence for a ethnic minority disposition towards colleges rather than schools.

Compared with whites, twice as many Afro-Caribbeans and four times as many Asians were taking 4 O level courses in the first post-compulsory year. The number of Asians was particularly high (one in five of the Asian cohort). This number dropped dramatically in the second post-compulsory year (to only one in twenty of the Asian cohort). A significant number of those who took O levels in the first year transferred to A levels in the second. I considered the hypothesis that Asians tended to repeat low level courses with little benefit to themselves, a view that was held by a number of careers officers in the study by Cross, Wrench and Barnett (1990). The data did not offer support for this position; some 'failed' but many others progressed on to higher level courses.

181

Ethnic minority young people, both Afro-Caribbean and Asian, were more likely to stay on than whites to take vocational qualifications. The success rates of all three groups were similar.

Studying A levels was still the most common choice at the post 16 stage. The number of Afro-Caribbean students pursuing this course of action at 16 was rather small, only 10 per cent of the cohort. This was in part due to the small number of Afro-Caribbeans who achieved four or more higher grade passes at 16. For those who did take A levels a multiple regression analysis showed that progress between the O level and the A level stage was similar for all ethnic groups; the weaker performance of the Afro-Caribbean group was largely a function of their weaker performance at the O level stage relative to the other groups. However, this analysis ignored those young people who either returned to education at a later stage or retook O levels before attempting A levels. This group was larger amongst ethnic minority students than amongst white and therefore the picture we have of academic attainment at 18 is incomplete as regards the eventual A level attainment of the ethnic minority cohort. Nevertheless, the small numbers of Afro-Caribbean students with A levels does give cause for concern.

A higher percentage of Afro-Caribbeans at 18 possessed vocational qualifications (NVQ levels 1, 2) than any other group whilst a higher percentage of Asians at 18 had passed two or more A levels than any other group. In general, then, ethnic minority groups were not short of educational qualifications, per se, although their profile was somewhat different overall from that of the white population. There would appear to have been considerable motivation towards academic or vocational achievement, a finding which is corroborated by qualitative studies (see Gillborn, 1990). This still begs the question of the extent to which Afro-Caribbean young people have been held back by their weaker fifth year performance. Since I found in my analysis that success or failure at this stage had a very strong effect on what happened later, this remains an important question. While one in four Asians and whites had obtained four or more O levels at 16 only one in ten Afro-Caribbean young people had done so. It was the lower proportions achieving the top levels which appeared to lead to Afro-Caribbeans choosing (or being channelled into) vocational courses rather than academic ones. Education has always been an important issue for ethnic minority communities, developing as they have from immigrant communities with strong interest in self-improvement (Sivanandan, 1982). Ethnic minority participation in post-compulsory education has been high and is likely to remain so.

In conclusion I should like to return to the general question about whether these findings reflect a continuity of trends found in the past and to what extent the findings reflect new differences which are beginning to emerge. The high participation rate in post-compulsory education reflects a continuing pattern and I was not altogether surprised to find this in my research. Other comparisons are more difficult because no other studies have analysed the post-compulsory period in as much detail as I did. What seems to be noteworthy is that the number of Afro-Caribbean young people with A levels is still somewhat low whilst there is a group of Asian young people with A levels which is a relatively large one. This progress is also reflected in entry to higher education. Since the route through higher education is the one which leads directly into managerial and professional occupations the numbers moving in this direction need to be carefully monitored. What is also clear is that within each ethnic group there are considerable numbers following each post-compulsory route; taking A levels, improving on O levels and taking vocational qualifications. We need to move away from oversimplified generalisations about 'underachievement' to recognise the diversity of these educational experiences. What is clear is that by the age of 19 ethnic minority young people have invested highly in educational qualifications. The next important question is whether these qualifications are given adequate recognition in the youth labour market.

The youth labour market

Transitional steps into the youth labour market have become considerably more complex in the last decade. 16 year-olds are faced with a potentially bewildering set of decisions.

The eighties witnessed a growth in general unemployment but also a growth in youth training; this ameliorated, to a certain extent, the effects of joblessness. Government intervention in the youth labour market therefore had a considerable effect. Ethnic minority young people seem to have benefited from this in a general sense, although previous research has raised the issue of the extent to which training schemes have been able to break free from the constraints and problems operating more generally in the labour market.

A major feature of my approach was to use statistical modelling procedure (logit models which are akin to multiple regression). This provides an important advance on previous studies of 'race' issues because it allowed me to control for a whole range of other individual-level variables (such as gender and social class) and some area characteristics (for example, local adult unemployment rates).

Before I can turn to the main findings a note of caution is required. The problem of survey non response and survey attrition was considered and this may have disproportionately affected Afro-Caribbean males in the survey; however, after undertaking a series of analyses I was also confident that it did not seriously affect my general findings. Comparisons with the Labour Force Survey suggested that unemployment rates may have been slightly underestimated as a result of low-qualified ethnic minority respondents not replying to later sweeps of the questionnaire; if this is the case, the situation for Afro-Caribbean males may have been somewhat worse than my analyses suggest.

Five major routes through the labour market from 16-19 were distinguished in this study; those taking two or more A levels (16 per cent), other full-time education (21 per cent), YTS (32 per cent), leaving school directly at 16 and finding a job ('traditional', 18 per cent) and other routes (12 per cent). These routes were treated as mutually exclusive; thus, if an individual went through YTS but also received some kind of full-time education, this individual was classified as having followed the YTS route. This classification of routes considerably simplifies how we think about the 16-19 year period; what I have done is to highlight the major routes followed by the survey respondents. In broad terms the education routes were favoured by Asians and the YTS route by Afro-Caribbeans (38 per cent followed this route compared with 33 per cent of whites and 17 per cent of Asians). However, very few ethnic minority young people moved directly into employment at 16 (only 8 per cent of Afro-Caribbeans and 5 per cent of Asians) compared with 19 per cent of white young people.

As well as considering the overall routes taken I examined what young people were doing at age 16 (at the beginning of the survey) and at age 19 (at the end of the survey). At 16, for those who entered the labour market, the major decision was whether to take up a job or a YTS place. About one half of all those not remaining in full-time education were to be found on YTS; there were about equal proportions of Afro-Caribbeans and whites but the numbers of Asians doing this was small (only one in ten of the whole cohort). These decisions were in part determined by attainment at 16 with the most academically competent students staying on in education. Since I have already shown that ethnic minority students were more likely to stay on than whites I found, not surprisingly, that those ethnic minority young people who entered the labour market were somewhat less well-qualified than their white counterparts.

In areas of high adult unemployment during the eighties some communities were heavily dependent on training opportunities; more young people were on training schemes there than in more prosperous areas. When considering such factors it is important to remember that for historical reasons, ethnic minority young people did not, on average, tend to be concentrated in areas of generally high adult unemployment at least in so far as these are captured by data on Travel to Work Areas. Their parents or grandparents settled in the fifties and sixties in areas where there was a demand for labour; these were areas of relatively full employment.

In modelling participation on YTS I found that Afro-Caribbean and working class young people were more likely to take up YTS places, having taken into account other factors including attainment at 16. When the local adult unemployment rate was added to this model it was found that the ethnic and social class differences were very much reduced. Put another way, local labour market conditions mediated the effects of ethnic differences; the odds of participation in YTS were 2.5 times higher in areas of high unemployment compared with areas of low unemployment, having taken into account attainment and ethnic origin. This model appears to provide strong evidence of demand side effects on YTS provision.

In analysing data on the unemployed, I felt the need to distinguish between those who were unemployed for short periods and those who were unemployed for longer ones. Whichever approach was taken, however, ethnic differences were found. The unemployment rates for ethnic minority groups at 16 were higher than for the white group. Unemployment was also strongly related to attainment; the low-qualified ethnic minority groups had much higher unemployment rates than any of the others. There was also more long term unemployment amongst ethnic minority young people. I found that those who had been on YTS schemes were more vulnerable to unemployment than those on some other routes but this, in a sense, was not surprising because YTS trainees were mainly those with middle to low academic attainments, the groups most likely to have had higher levels of unemployment.

Modelling the probability of unemployment at 16 demonstrated that gender, attainment and ethnic origin were major factors. For those who left school at this stage there were large differences between groups. Taking two fairly extreme examples, white males with high attainment had only a 7 per cent chance of unemployment whilst Asian males with low attainment had a 35 per cent chance.

Modelling the probability of unemployment 19 produced results showing that the same factors were significant. In addition, social class, parental education and the route taken by young people into the labour market were also of importance. If, for example, we take those who used the YTS route, who also possessed 1-3 higher grade passes and had non-graduate parents, striking differences are found. White males with professional parents were estimated to have an unemployment rate of just 8 per cent; Afro-Caribbean females with parents in manual occupations were estimated to have an unemployment rate of 27 per cent. These estimates were, of course, at the extremes but they suggest the existence of several factors in operation over and above the route taken and the qualifications achieved.

The analysis was completed by considering employment at 19. This was done because having a job does represent what most people would judge to be 'success' in the youth labour market. It is, of course, only a crude measure of such success because job quality, pay and hours worked were not teased out in this analysis. What I was able to show was that attainment of academic or vocational qualifications, in combination with the route taken into the labour market, were crucial determinants of success. This came as no surprise. What was also found was that, over and above this, social class, gender, parental education and ethnic origin were also of some importance in determining the outcomes.

Ethnic minority young people were not, according to the YCS evidence, finding their way successfully into the labour market. At the age of 19, 66 per cent of whites were in jobs, 56 per cent of Afro-Caribbeans and just 30 per cent of Asians. Whilst this was in part due to the apparent enthusiasm ethnic minority young people had for educational opportunities, it was also due to other factors as well. When I modelled the probability of being in employment at 19 this became clear.

Using the model results I was able to compare individuals with the same attainment, route and parental education. For example, I took those with 1-3 higher grade passes, who had taken the YTS route and had non graduate parents. This model excluded those still in full-time education. For white males from professional backgrounds the probability of being in employment was 84 per cent; for Afro-Caribbean males with parents in manual occupations the probability of

186

being in employment was 70 per cent and for Asian females with parents in manual occupations the probability was 51 per cent.

The research conducted here allows us to address two important issues that have been prominent in research on race. The first is the educational 'underachievement' of ethnic minority young people; the second the continuation of racial discrimination in the youth labour market. On the first issue it was found that the Afro-Caribbean group was lagging behind the other groups; by exactly how much and whether this should be judged as considerable depended to some extent on which measure of qualifications was employed. This factor should not, however, overshadow the education progress that was being made by ethnic minority young people. The Asian group was performing as well as the white group at the O level stage and sizeable numbers of Afro-Caribbeans and Asians were obtaining academic and vocational qualifications in the post 16 period. On the other hand I also found that, whatever the level of educational attainment, there were barriers to progress for ethnic minority young people; Afro-Caribbeans and Asians were more likely to become unemployed and less likely to find full-time jobs. Racial discrimination has, during the last two decades, been shown to be a major factor in the labour market and, in the absence of other explanations of the differences I have found, these analyses suggest that this continues to be the case.

An agenda for future research

The purpose of this concluding section is to make comments on future research and consider some wider trends in statistical research on ethnic minorities. In 1978 I became involved in research on 'race' and ethnicity whilst teaching at Sheffield Polytechnic. I approached Ushar Prashar, the Director of the Runnymede Trust offering to help improve their presentation of statistics. The collaboration was a fruitful one and led in 1980 to the publication with a number of authors of the book 'Britain's Black Population', a joint publication with the Radical Statistics Race Group (Runnymede Trust and Radical Statistics Race Group, 1980). This book was the first statistical review of 'race', demography, education, employment, health, housing, social services and the politics of 'race' data collection and became a popular undergraduate reader with over 10,000 copies sold. The contents of the book are still highly relevant today; achievement in education, unemployment, discrimination, social disadvantage and poverty.

Given the 15 years between that publication and this one this seems, in some senses, depressing. The question keeps coming back; what has changed? If the answer is that not much has changed this suggests that research on achievement and unemployment will continue to be important. This does not mean, however, that no new lines of research are required. There are also new trends that it will be important to monitor and new ways to conceptualise issues and analyse data.

One of the most promising recent developments is the ready availability of large data sets from government departments for secondary analysis. Improvements both in documentation and availability on the Internet and the mean that the burden of getting started with data analysis has been considerably lightened. Data sets which could provide continuing analyses of education and youth labour market trends include the Youth Cohort Study, the 1991 Population Census, and the Labour Force Survey. More work needs to be done to make use of the continuing nature of such surveys to monitor change over time. With the inclusion of an ethnic question in the Census for the first time, the 1991 Population Census provides a further opportunity to examine ethnic differences and the availability of a 2 per cent sample of anonymised records of individuals (the SARs) has provided the largest nationally representative survey data set of its kind to date, with over a million records.

The potential for ethnic analyses of this data has already been explored (Ballard and Kalfa, 1994; Drew and Fosam, 1994; Forrest and Gordon, 1993; Owen, 1992 and 1993; Rees, Phillips and Medway, 1993; Simpson, 1993) and 4 volumes of analysis are due to be published in 1995 by OPCS. This new interest by government departments should be warmly welcomed and the analyses produced will provide an essential benchmark until the next Census in 2001.

A second change in approaches to research will be the level of data analysis. In some senses Afro-Caribbean and Asian young people have a common experience of racism but it will be important for future statistical research to focus on particular groups to examine differences between them. The Asian group needs to be differentiated for example to take into account the different experiences of Indian young people and those from Pakistani and Bangladeshi backgrounds. There is a tendency to polarisation in terms of class position and occupational level; the ethnic minority middle class will continue to grow whilst the problems of the less skilled and the unemployed will deepen. This needs to be further studied.

Improvements in large nationally representative data sets should make such comparisons easier. Enhancements to the Labour Force Survey in 1992 mean that more detailed analyses and comparisons could be routinely made and published by the Employment Department. This could include more detailed analyses of existing indicators, for example, a breakdown of unemployment by ethnic origin, gender and socio-economic group to identify the kind of polarisation just discussed. It could also routinely include new analyses, for example, of income since differences in income levels by ethnic group, socio-economic group and educational qualifications could become increasingly interesting as progress towards equality (or not) is made.

Further progress needs to be made in the way statistical research in this area is conceptualised. In the Eighties there was a strong focus on underachievement. This implicitly or explicitly laid blame on the 'victim', the young people themselves. Recent research using the 1991 Census (Drew and Fosam, 1994) shows a number of ethnic groups outperforming whites in examination attainment, yet with high unemployment rates which suggests that achievement is a necessary but not sufficient condition for getting a job (see Figure. 7.1). There has been and should continue to be a shift towards research on occupational attainment, that is measuring the differences between groups in the returns on their investments in education. This book is a contribution to this style of research.

Anthony Heath and colleagues at Oxford have also contributed to this (Cheng and Heath, 1994; Heath and McMahon, 1994). Their research shows that progress into the service class (the professional and managerial class) after controlling for attainment and age differences is slower for ethnic minority groups than for whites. The ethnic differences, after taking attainment and age into account, are described as 'ethnic penalties'. They have shown that the Indian group appears to have a reasonably large number in the service class but, after controlling for attainment and age, 'ethnic penalties' appear for this group also. Thus we have certain groups, for example the Bangladeshis, which appear to be doing very badly in the labour market and other groups, for example the Indians, who appear to be doing relatively well but for whom there is still cause for concern. Further research is needed to show how much of this 'ethnic penalty' is due to direct and indirect discrimination in the labour market and how much is due to other causes.

A further recent development is the debate about the meanings and boundaries of research on ethnicity and in particular the difficulty of

189

establishing the importance of racism as a factor. My own critique (with David Gillborn) of the book 'The School Effect' (Smith and Tomlinson, 1989) is a case in point (see Gillborn and Drew, 1992). We argued that the importance of racism in the lives of the school children in this book was under researched. Furthermore we were worried by the interpretation of their findings that the 'school a child goes to makes far more difference than which ethnic group he or she belongs to' (Smith and Tomlinson, 1989:281) and the conclusion that 'the measures that will most help the racial minorities are the same as those that will raise the standards of secondary education generally' (1989:281). If the intention of this book had been to provide copy for reactionary pundits and certain sections of the media, it succeeded brilliantly. Ray Honeyford commented that 'the report is a damning reversal of everything the race relations industry has pumped out about ethnic children's educational prospects in this country' (R.Honeyford, Daily Mail, 9 June 1989) and the Sunday Times carried a banner headline that 'Race is No Longer an Educational Factor'.

As it turned out Smith and Tomlinson's findings were at best provisional, used a fairly crude multi-level model, was based on a very small sample by current standards and did not address important questions about the extent to which ethnic minority young people were attending schools in which the average progress of pupils was slow. Our own critique was in turn attacked (Hammersley and Gomm, 1993) and Barry Troyna's research also (Hammersley, 1992). Whilst we strongly argue (Gillborn and Drew, 1993) that their criticisms misrepresent our position we accept that the problem of establishing the relative importance racism plays in determining the life chances of ethnic minority young people, as against other factors, is a difficult one. Interestingly, these authors (Hammersley and Gomm, 1993) do not take issue with any of the statistical points made in our original comments on 'The School Effect' and they comment almost wholly on issues of qualitative research which they obviously regard as a softer target.

Hammersley's latest criticisms (1995) group together a number of researchers (including myself) working in this area, describes us as 'antiracists' and stereotypes our position and motives. He argues that research should return to being 'value neutral', an old argument based on a naive, idealized and ideological understanding of the way research in natural science and social science is conducted.

The question of the meanings and boundaries of research on ethnicity and 'race' is now being discussed more fully in the academic

190

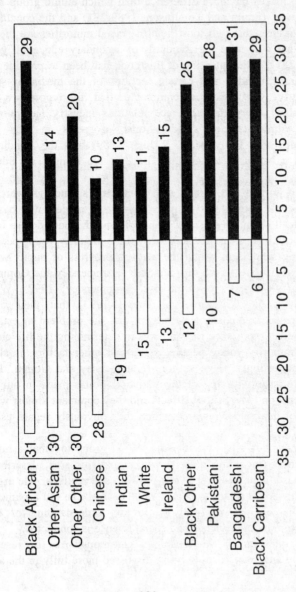

Figure 7.1 Percentage qualified and percentage unemployed, males aged 18 and over by ethnic group

Source: 1991 Population Census, Great Britain

literature. The apparent over representation of Afro-Caribbean males in crime is a serious cause for concern (see Carr-Hill and Drew, 1988). Marian Fitzgerald has discussed the problem of establishing the phenomenon of racism in such research and her comments raise important issues about the difficulties involved (Fitzgerald, 1993). In the United States whole books are written on the subject of ethnicity and research methods (Stanfield and Dennis, 1993).

The treatment of 'race', gender and social class is also an issue of conceptual importance. It has been the purpose of this book to integrate these three dimensions in the analysis and these social cleavages will continue to be important for the foreseeable future (Fieldhouse, 1994). Research on social class differences in education have been with us for some time (see Heath and Clifford, 1990; and Paterson, 1992) but other researchers (Tizard et al, 1988) have pointed out that it is relatively rare to analyse 'race', gender and social class differences in a single study either in the US or in Britain. The interaction of 'race', gender and social class has yet to be fully explored. The worlds of working class, ethnic minority young women and middle class white young men are very different. Such a point seems hardly controversial and yet this is not reflected in statistical research. Whilst this is the case we will continue to have analyses which generalise about ethnic minority groups as though they are homogeneous when, of course, they are not.

One further trend is that future studies will undoubtedly make more use of similarities and differences between our situation in Britain and that in other parts of the world, in different parts of Europe and in the United States in particular. Not surprisingly, similar research on 'race', education and the labour market is common in the US (Lobo, 1993; Thomas, 1993 and Wilson, 1987). Yuan Cheng has made a comparison in occupational attainments of the Chinese in Britain and the Chinese in the US and this study should provide a model for future work (Cheng, 1994).

The development of equal opportunities practice in the Eighties has been depressingly slow and the 1976 Race Relations Act has been relatively ineffective in tackling institutional discrimination (see McCrudden et al, 1991). The call by the CRE for compulsory ethnic record keeping and monitoring is unlikely to be met with a favourable response. The availability of statistical data on equality targets and ethnic monitoring is likely therefore to be limited. It is challenging to learn that, in a recent study by the International Labour Office the UK was considered to be one of the front runners in the development of anti-discrimination legislation (Zegers de Beijl, 1991). There are current fears about the rise of racism and xenophobia in Europe and the decade of the Nineties will see a move towards greater mobility of labour within the European community. These trends will mean that international comparisons of the experiences of ethnic minority young people in the labour market will increasingly be of interest.

It has been argued that whilst government publications emphasise good employment practices government policies elsewhere create a climate where the chances of success are reduced (see Wrench, 1993). The responsibility for youth training has now moved from the Employment Department to the Training and Enterprise Councils (TECs). This has raised fears that even the limited progress made on equal opportunities will be dissipated. The effect of this on ethnic minority young people in youth training and the use by the TECs of the Ethnic Minority Grant to meet the training needs of ethnic minority young people should be studied.

Government policies in education may also disproportionately affect ethnic minority young people. The National Curriculum puts very little emphasis on other cultures and multicultural input continues to be largely at the level of rhetoric (Tomlinson, 1991). Equality of educational opportunity will, however, continue to be at the heart of much research and debate. For this reason analyses of the progress of children which take into account both the characteristics of the child and the characteristics of the school will remain of importance. Such multi-level analyses should become more routinely available as the data bases produced by schools and local education authorities are improved. It should therefore become possible to assess more fully the contribution that schools make to the different progress of ethnic minority and white children.

It is interesting, in conclusion, to look back a quarter of a century to the first PEP study, from which the quote at the beginning of the chapter was taken (Daniel, 1968). In the analysis of the Youth Cohort Study data I have found that, at all levels of educational attainment, job finding is more difficult for ethnic minority young people than for whites. This was true in 1968.

Applied to a public office for a job. I was given a job behind the scenes and not allowed to mix with the public. It was said in my presence that the public did not like coloured people. So I was not given a clerical officer's job although I am a graduate and am better educated than my superiors.

(Daniel, 1968 : 75)

193

The difference then was that employers were more open about their racism. One employer who did not employ ethnic minority people at any level said: 'The Managing Director is prejudiced and so am I. If one came here for a job we'd just say there was no vacancy.' (Daniel, 1968 : 99). Another employer was more forceful: 'I don't like blacks, I don't employ blacks and I don't want to talk about blacks.' (Daniel, 1968 : 99). Now, a quarter of a century later it is rare to hear such openly held views and yet the statistical evidence of discrimination is still clear. One can understand the pessimism of some ethnic minority young people about progress towards equality. One wonders how much has really changed.

It is depressing to see the emergence in 1994 of 'The Bell Curve' by Herrnstein and Murray, on 'race' and IQ differences in the United States. They take 845 pages to argue that almost every social problem, poverty, unemployment, idleness, illegitimacy, crime and welfare dependency stems from low IQ. The hypotheses are historically implausible, there is little new in the book that was not written 20 years ago, the analysis is deeply flawed and the policy conclusions are extremely reactionary.

To end this analysis on such a negative note would however be wrong. My own book has a rather different set of hypotheses, analyses and conclusions to those of Herrnstein and Murray. The premise here is that human potential is extraordinarily widely distributed in the population and it is the accident of birth, of 'race', place, gender and class that is at the centre of inequality. These inequalities are not natural and preordained properties of the Universe, they are socially constructed and maintain the dominance of one 'race' and class by another.

The goal of education is to help liberate human potential in the individual in order to create wisdom, harmony and progress. The power to realise this lies in the hands both of the individual and those who decide policy. Ethnic minority young people in Britain are making the most of their opportunities, in diverse and exciting ways and it is the responsibility of those involved in deciding education and employment policy to make the right opportunities available. The young people themselves can be relied upon to do the rest. We owe it to them that the next generation does not suffer the same frustrations as the last. As Aimé Cesaire wrote: 'No race holds the monopoly of beauty, of intelligence, of strength and there is a place for all at the rendezvous of victory'.

194

References

Ballard, R. and Kalfa, V. (1994) 'The Ethnic Dimensions of the 1991 Census: A preliminary report', University of Manchester: Census Microdata Unit.

Banks, M., Ullah, P. and Warr, P. (1986) *Unemployment and less qualified urban young people*, Department of Employment Gazette, 92(8): 340-346, London: HMSO.

Benedict, R. (1983) *Race or Racism*, London: Routledge and Kegan Paul.

Booth, H., (1988). 'Identifying ethnic origin', in A Bhat, R. Carr-Hill and S. Ohri (eds.) *Britain's Black Population*, Aldershot: Gower Press, pp. 237 - 266.

Brah, A. K. and Golding, P. (1983) *The Transition from School to Work among Young Asians in Leicester*, University of Leicester.

Brah, A. and Shaw, S. (1992) *Working Choices: South Asian Young Muslim Women and the Labour Market*, Sheffield: Employment Department Research Paper No. 91 (pp. 69).

Brennan, J. and McGeevor, P. (1987) *Employment of Graduates from Ethnic Minorities*, London: Commission for Racial Equality.

Brooks, D. (1975) *Race and Labour in London Transport*, Oxford University Press.

Brown, A. and Behrens, M. (1990) *'Routes to skilled work in England and the Federal Republic of Germany'*. Paper presented at the Annual Conference of the British Educational Research Association (London: Roehampton Institute).

Brown, C. (1984) *Black and White Britain: The Third PSI Survey*, London: Heinemann/Gower for Policy Studies Institute.

Brown, C. (1990) Racial inequality in the British labour market, *Employment Institute Economic Report*, Vol.5, No.4, June 1990.

Brown, C. (1992) 'Same difference. The persistence of racial disadvantage in the British employment market,' in P. Braham et al (eds.) *Racism and Anti-Racism : Inequalities, Opportunities and Policies*, London: Sage Publications, pp. 46-63.

Brown, C. and Gay, P. (1985) *Racial Discrimination : 17 years after the Act*, London: Policy Studies Institute.

Burnhill, P., Garner, C. and McPherson, A. (1990) 'Parental Education, Social Class and Entry to Higher Education' 1976-86, *J.R. Statist. Soc.* A, 153, Part 2, 233-248.

Bussue, L. and Drew, D. (1985) *Sheffield's Black Population: Employment*, Research Report AS/7, Sheffield City Polytechnic (pp.59).

Byford, D. and Mortimore, P. (1985) *School Examination Results in the ILEA 1984*, RS 977/85, London: Inner London Education Authority.

Carmichael, S. and Hamilton, C.V. (1968) *Black Power: The Politics of Liberation in America*, London: Jonathan Cape.

Carr-Hill, R and Drew, D (1988) 'Blacks, Police and Crime' in Bhat, A. et al (eds) *Britain's Black Population - A New Perspective*, Gower Press, 29-60.

Castles, S and Kosack, G. (1973) *Immigrant Workers and Class Structure in Western Europe*, London: Oxford University Press.

Centre for Contemporary Cultural Studies (1982) *The Empire Strikes Back*, London: Hutchinson.

Cheng, Y. (1994) *Education and Class: Chinese in Britain and the US*, Aldershot: Avebury.

Cheng, Y. and Heath, A (1993) 'Ethnic origins and class destinations' *Oxford Review of Education*, vol, 19, No. 2, 151-165.

Clough, E. and Drew D.with Wojciechowski, A. (1985) *Futures in Black and White: Two Studies of the Experiences of Young People in Sheffield and Bradford*, Sheffield: Pavic Publications.

Clough, E., Drew, D. and Jones, B. (1988) 'Ethnic differences in the youth labour market in Bradford and Sheffield', *New Community*, 14, 412-425.

Cohen, P. (1992) 'Hidden narratives in the theories of racism', in J. Donald and A. Rattansi (eds.) `Race', Culture and Difference*, London, Sage Publications, pp. 62-103.

Commission for Racial Equality (1978) *Looking for Work: London Black and White School Leavers in Lewisham*, London: CRE.

Commission for Racial Equality (1986) *Review of the Race Relations Act, 1976: Proposals for Change*, London: CRE.

Commission for Racial Equality (1987) *Formal Investigation: Chartered Accountancy Training Contracts*, London: CRE.

Connolly, M., Roberts, K., Ben-Tovim, G. and Torkington, P. (1992) *Black Youth in Liverpool*, Giordano Bruno Culemborg.

Courtenay, G. (1989a) *England and Wales Youth Cohort Study: Report on Cohort 2 Sweep 1*, Sheffield: Training Agency Research and Development Series No. 48.

Courtenay, G. (1989b) *England and Wales Youth Cohort Study: Report on Cohort 3 Sweep 1*, Sheffield: Training Agency Research and Development Series No. 53.

Courtenay, G. (1990a) *England and Wales Youth Cohort Study: Report on Cohort 2 Sweep 2*, Sheffield: Training Agency Research and Development Series No. 55.

Courtenay, G. (1990b) *England and Wales Youth Cohort Study: Report on Cohort 2 Sweep 3*, Sheffield: Training Agency Research and Development Series No. 59.

Craft, M. and Craft, A. (1983) 'The participation of ethnic minority pupils in further and higher education', *Educational Research*, 25, 1, 10-19.

Cross, M., Edmonds, J. and Sargeant, R. (1983) *Special Problems and Special Measures: Ethnic Minorities and the Experiences of YOP*, Manpower Services Commission Special Programmes Occasional Paper No. 5., Sheffield: MSC.

Cross, M. and Smith, D. (1987) *Black Youth Futures: Ethnic Minorities and the Youth Training Scheme*, Leicester: National Youth Bureau.

Cross, M., Wrench, J. and Barnett, S. (1990) *Ethnic Minorities and the Careers Service: An Investigation into Processes of Assessment and Placement*, Department of Employment Research Paper Series No. 73.

Cross, M. and Wrench J. (1991) 'Processing black youngsters for YTS: Careers service or disservice?', *British Journal of Education and Work*, 4, 3, 5-23.

Daniel, W. W. (1968) *Racial Discrimination in England*, Harmondsworth: Penguin.

Department of Education and Science (1985) *Education for All* (The Swann Report), London: HMSO.

Department of Employment (1987) *Employment Gazette*, January 1987.

Department of Employment (1990) 'Ethnic origins and the labour market', *Employment Gazette*, March 1990.

Drew, D. (1972) 'The dependence of A-level examination performance on observed social factors and school characteristics'. MSc dissertation (unpublished). University of Birmingham, Department of Mathematical Statistics (pp. 124).

Drew, D. (1981) *A Classification of Residential Neighbourhoods of Sheffield using Cluster Analysis*, Research Report MS/23, Sheffield City Polytechnic. (pp.26).

Drew, D. (1986) *Statistics and anti-racist strategies*, Research Report AS/9, Sheffield City Polytechnic, (pp.70).

Drew, D. (1993) The Education and labour market experiences of black young people in England and Wales. PhD Thesis, University of Sheffield.

Drew, D. and Bussue, L. (1985) 'Sheffield's Black Population: Employment', Research Report AS/7, Sheffield City Polytechnic.

Drew, D and Fosam, B. (1994) 'Gender and ethnic differences in education and the youth labour market'. *Radical Statistics*, No. 58 (pp16-35).

Drew, D. and Gray, J. (1990) 'The fifth year examination achievements of black young people in England and Wales', *Educational Research*, 32, 2, 107-117.

Drew, D. and Gray, J. (1991) 'The black-white gap in exam achievement: a statistical critique of a decade's research', *New Community*, 17,2.

Drew, D., Gray, J. and Sime, N. (1992) 'Against the Odds: The Education and Labour Market Experiences of Black Young People', Sheffield: Employment Department Training Research and Development Series, No. 68 - *Youth Cohort Series No. 19* (pp. 56).

Drew, D., Gray, J. and Sporton, D. (1995) 'Ethnic Differences in the educational participation of 16-19 year olds' To be published in OPCS volume on ethnic minorities and the 1991 Population Census edited by V Karn.

Drew, D., Okell, E. and Wisher, S. (1988) *The Sheffield Equal Opportunities Survey of Nurses*, Research Report SU/1, Sheffield City Polytechnic (pp.70).

Driver, G. (1980) *Beyond Under-Achievement*, London: Commission for Racial Equality.

Eggleston, S.J., Dunn, D.K., Anjali, M. and Wright, C. (1986) *Education for Some: The Educational and Vocational Experience of 15-18 year old Members of Minority Ethnic Groups*, Stoke on Trent: Trentham Books.

198

Evans, K. and Heinz, W. R. (1990) 'Career Trajectories', paper presented at the Annual Conference of the British Educational Research Association (London, Roehampton Institute).

Fenton, S., Davies, T., Means R. and Burton, P. (1984) *Ethnic Minorities and the Youth Training Scheme*, MSC Research and Development Paper No. 20, Sheffield: MSC.

Field, S., (1981) *Ethnic Minorities In Britain: A Study of Trends in their Position Since 1961*, London: HMSO.

Fieldhouse, E. and Tye, R. (1994) 'Deprived people or deprived places? Explaining the ecological fallacy in studies of deprivation using the Samples of Anonymised Records. Census Microdata Unit: Manchester University. Submitted for publication.

Fitzgerald, M. (1993) 'Racism: Establishing the Phenomenon' in D. Cook and B. Hudson (eds) *Racism and Criminology*, London: Sage Publications.

Forrest, R. and Gordon, G. (1993) *People and Places: A 1991 Census Atlas of England*. Bristol: School for Advanced Urban Studies.

Fryer, P (1987) 'Pseudo-Scientific Racism', in D Gill and L Levidow (eds.) *Anti-Racist Science Teaching*, London: Free Association Books.

Garner, C., Main, B. and Raffe, D. (1988) 'The distribution of school leaver unemployment within Scottish cities', *Urban Studies* 25: 133-144.

Gibbon, P. (1990) 'Equal opportunity policy and race equality', *Critical Social Policy*, Issue 28, Vol 10, No 1, 5-24.

Gill, D and Levidow, L. (1987) *Anti-racist science teaching*, London: Free Association Books

Gillborn, D. (1990) `Race', Ethnicity and Education: Teaching and Learning in Multi-Ethnic Schools*, London: Unwin Hynam.

Gillborn, D. and Drew, D. (1992) 'Race, Class and School Effects', *New Community*, 18(4): 551-565.

Gillborn, D. and Drew, D. (1993) 'The politics of research: some observations on 'methodological purity' ', *New Community*, 19(2): 355-361.

Gilroy, P. (1987) *There Aint No Black in the Union Jack*, London: Hutchinson.

Gilroy, P. (1992) 'The end of anti-racism' in J. Donald and A. Rattansi (eds.) `Race', Culture and Difference*, London: Sage Publications, pp. 49-61.

Goldstein, H. (1987) *Multi-level Models in Social and Educational Research*, London: Griffin Press.

199

Gordon, A. (1981) 'The educational choices of young people', in O. Fulton (ed.) *Access to Higher Education*, Guildford: Society for Research into Higher Education.

Gray, J., Jesson, D. and Sime, N. (1990) 'Estimating Differences in the Examination Performances of Secondary Schools in Six LEAs: a Multi-level Approach to School Effectiveness', *Oxford Review of Education*, 16, 2, 137-158.

Gray, J. and Pattie, C. (1988) *Getting Better Qualified? The Position at 17-plus*, Educational Research Centre, Sheffield University.

Gray, J. and Sime, N. (1990) *Patterns of Participation in Full-Time Post-Compulsory Education*, Sheffield: Training Agency Research and Development Series.

Gurnah, A. (1987) 'Gatekeepers and caretakers : Swann, Scarman and the social policy of containment', in B. Troyna (ed.) *Racial Inequality in Education*, London: Tavistock.

Hall, S. (1992a) 'New ethnicities', in J. Donald and A. Rattansi (eds.), `Race', Culture and Difference*, London: Sage Publications, pp. 252-259.

Hall, S. (1992b) 'The West and the Rest: Discourse and Power,' in S. Hall and B. Gieben (eds.) *Formations of Modernity*, Oxford: Polity Press, pp. 276-320.

Hall, S. (1992c) 'The Question of Cultural Identity' in S. Hall, D. Held and T. McGrew (eds.) *Modernity and Its Futures*, Oxford: Polity Press, pp. 274-316.

Hammersley, M. (1995) *The Politics of Social Research*, London: Sage Publications.

Hammersley, M (1992) 'A response to Barry Troyna's 'Children, race and racism': The limits of research and policy', *British Journal of Educational Studies*, 40 (2): 174-187.

Hammersley, M. and Gomm, R. (1993) 'A response to Gillborn and Drew on 'Race, Class and School Effects', *New Community,* 19 (2).

Hardy, J. and Vieler-Porter, C. (1993) 'Race, schooling and the Education Reform Act', in D Gill, B Mayor and M. Blair (eds) *Racism and Education: Structures and Strategies*, London: Sage Publications, pp. 101-114.

Heath, A. (1981) *Social Mobility*, London: Fontana.

Heath, A. and Clifford, P. (1990) 'Class inequalities in education in the twentieth century', *J R Statist. Soc A*, 153, Part 1, pp1-16.

Heath, A. and McMahon, D. (1994) 'Education and occupational attainments: the impact of ethnic origins'. Paper presented to the

OPCS/ESRC Census Analysis Group Conference on the Census Ethnic Volumes held at the University of Leeds, September 1994.

Herrnstein, R. and Murray, C. (1994) *The Bell Curve*, New York, Free Press.

Hubbuck, I. and Carter, S. (1980) *Half a Chance: a Report on Job Discrimination amongst Young Blacks in Nottingham*, Nottingham CRC/CRE.

Inner London Education Authority (1990) 'Differences in examination performance', *ILEA Research and Statistics*, RS 1277/90.

Jenkins, R. (1992) 'Black workers in the labour market', in P. Braham, A. Rattansi and R. Skellington (eds.) *Racism and AntiRacism - Inequalities, Opportunities and Policies*, London: Sage Publications.

Jesson, D., Gray, J. and Sime, N. (1991) *Participation, Progress and Performance in Post-Compulsory Education*, Sheffield: Training Agency Research and Development series.

Jewson, N., Mason, D., Lambkin, C. and Taylor, F. (1992) *Ethnic Monitoring Policy and Practice: A Study of Employer's Experiences*, Sheffield: Employment Department Research Paper No. 89 (pp. 150).

Johnes, G. and Taylor, J. (1989) *Ethnic minorities in the graduate labour market*, New Community 15(4): 527-536.

Jones, T. (1993) *Britain's Ethnic Minorities*, London: Policy Studies Institute.

Kysel, F. (1988) 'Ethnic Background and Examination Results', *Educational Research*, 30 (2).

Lansley, S., Goss, S. and Wolmar, C. (1989) *Councils in Conflict, The Rise and Fall of the Municipal Left*. London: Macmillan.

Lee, V.E. and Smith, J.B. (1989) 'Gender Equality in teachers' salary: a multi-level approach', paper presented at the ESRC International Conference on Multi-level Methods in Educational Research (University of Edinburgh).

Lobo, P (1993) 'Are the streets paved with gold? An examination of the socio-economic outcomes of Asian and Latino immigrants to the United States', Research report no. 93-282, Population Studies Centre, University of Michigan.

Mabey, C. (1986) 'Black Pupils' Achievements in Inner London', *Educational Research*, 28 (3).

Mac an Ghaill, M. (1988) *Young, Gifted and Black*, Milton Keynes: Open University Press.

Mac an Ghaill, M. (1989) 'Coming-of-age in 1980's England: reconceptualising black students' schooling experience', *British Journal of Sociology of Education*, 10,3, 273-286.

Mason, D. (1990) 'A Rose by any other name....? Categorisation, Identity and Social Science', *New Community*, 17, 1: 123-133.

Maughan, B. and Rutter, M. (1986) 'Black pupils' progress in secondary schools II: examination achievements', *British Journal of Developmental Psychology*, 4, 19-29.

McCrudden, C. et al (1991) *Racial Justice at Work: Enforcement of the Race Relations Act, 1976, in Employment*, London: PSI.

Micklewright, J., Pearson M. and Smith, S. (1990) 'Unemployment and early School Leaving', *The Economic Journal*, 100, 163-169.

Middleton, B. J. (1983) `Factors Affecting the Performance of West Indian Boys in a Secondary School', M.A. Thesis, University of York.

Miles, R (1989) *Racism*, London and New York:Routledge.

Mirza, H. S. (1992) *Young, Female and Black*, Routledge.

Modood, T. (1988) 'Black', racial equality and Asian identity, *New Community*, 14 (3): 397-404.

Modood, T. (1992) *Not Easy Being British: Colour, Culture and Citizenship*, Stoke on Trent: Trentham Books.

Myers, S. (1993) 'Measuring and detecting discrimination in the post civil rights era', in J. Stanfield and R. Dennis (eds), *Race and Ethnicity in Research Methods*, London: Sage Publications.

Nuttall, D., Goldstein, H., Prosser, R., and Rasbash, J. (1989) 'Differential School Effectiveness', *International Journal of Educational Research*, 13: 769-776.

Ohri, S. and Faruqi, S. (1988) 'Racism, employment and unemployment', in A Bhat, R Carr-Hill and S Ohri (eds) *Britain's Black Population*, Aldershot: Gower.

Ouseley, H. (1982) *The System*, A Runnymede Trust and South London Equal Rights Consultancy Publication.

Ouseley, H. (1993) 'Resisting institutional change', in D Gill, B Mayor and M. Blair (eds) *Racism and Education: Structures and Strategies*, London: Sage Publications, pp. 119-133.

Owen, D. (1992) 'Ethnic Minorities in Great Britain: Settlement Patterns', 1991 Census Statistical Paper No. 1, Warwick University: Centre for Research in Ethnic Relations.

Owen, D. and Green, A (1992) 'Labour market experience and occupational change amongst ethnic groups in Great Britain', *New Community* 19(1): 7-29.

Owen, D, (1993) 'The spatial variations in ethnic minority populations in Great Britain'. Paper presented at a conference, Research on the 1991 Census, University of Newcastle, 13-15 September, 1993.

Parekh, B. (1983) 'Educational opportunity in multi-ethnic Britain', in N. Glazer and K. Young, (eds.), *Ethnic Pluralism and Public Policy*, London: Heinemann Educational Books.

Parekh, B. (1993) 'The hermeneutics of the Swann Report' in D Gill, B Mayor and M. Blair (eds) *Racism and Education: Structures and Strategies*, London: Sage Publications, pp. 92-100.

Paterson, L. (1992) 'The Influence of Opportunity on Aspirations amongst prospective university entrants from Scottish schools, 1970-88', *J R Statist. Soc A*, 155, Part 1, pp37-60.

Patrinos, H. and Sakellariou, C. (1991) 'North American Indians and wage discrimination in the Canadian labour market'. Paper presented at the British Sociological Association Annual Conference, Manchester 25-28 March.

Penn, R. and Scattergood, H. (1992) 'Ethnicity and career aspirations in contemporary Britain', *New Community* 19(1): 75-98.

Pirani, M., Yolles, M. and Bassa, E. (1992) 'Ethnic pay differentials', *New Community* 19(1): 31-42.

Plewis, I. (1987) 'Social disadvantage, educational attainment and ethnicity : a comment', *British Journal of Sociology of Education*, 8, 1, 77-81.

Plewis, I. (1988) 'Assessing and understanding the educational progress of children from different ethnic groups', *J. R. Statistical Society*, 151: Part 2.

Raffe, D. and Williams, J.D. (1989) 'Schooling the discouraged worker: local labour-market effects on educational participation', *Sociology*, 23, 4, 559-581.

Rees, P. , Phillips, D. and Medway, D. (1993) 'The Socio-economic Position of Ethnic Minorities in two Northern Cities.' Paper presented at a conference, Research on the 1991 Census, University of Newcastle, 13-15 September 1993.

Rex, J. (1973) *Race, Colonialism and the City*, London: Oxford University Press.

Rex, J. and Mason, D. (1986) *Theories of Race and Ethnic Relations*, Cambridge: Cambridge University Press.

Rex, J. and Moore, R. (1967) *Race, Community and Conflict*, London: Oxford University Press.

Richardson, R. (1992) 'Race policies under attack : two case studies for the 1990s', in D. Gill, B. Mayor and M. Blair (eds.) *Racism and Education: Structures and Strategies*, London: Sage Publications, pp. 134-150.

Roberts, K., Noble, M. and Duggan, J. (1983) 'Young, black and out of work', in B. Troyna et al (ed.) *Racism, School and the Labour Market*, Leicester: National Youth Bureau.

Robinson, P. (1990) 'Racial disadvantage and the economic cycle', *Campaign for Work Research Report*, Vol. 2, No. 5, July 1990.

Robinson, V. (1988) 'The new Indian middle class in Britain', *Ethnic and Racial Studies* Volume 11, Number 4, 456-473.

Robinson, V. (1990) 'Roots to mobility: the social mobility of Britain's black population', 1971-87, *Ethnic and Racial Studies*, Volume 13, Number 2, 1990.

Rodney, W (1972) *How Europe Underdeveloped Africa*, London: Bogle-L`Ouverture Publications.

Runnymede Trust and Radical Statistics Race Group (1980) *Britain's Black Population*, London: Heinemann Educational Books.

Scott, D. (1990) *School Experiences and Career Aspirations of Afro-Caribbean 16-30 Year Olds*, CEDAR, University of Warwick.

Shaw, C. (1988) 'Latest estimates of ethnic minority populations: Great Britain 1984-6', *Population Trends*, 51, 5-8.

Sillitoe, K. (1978) 'Ethnic Origins 1,2,3,' Office of Population Censuses and Surveys Occasional Papers 8,9,10 respectively, London: HMSO.

Sillitoe, K. and Meltzer, H. (1985) *The West Indian School Leaver*, Volumes 1 and 2, OPCS/HMSO, London.

Sime, N. and Gray, J. (1990) 'Youth Cohort Study', *Labour Market Quarterly Report*, May 1990.

Sime, N., Pattie, C. and Gray, J. (1990) *What Now? The Transition from School to the Labour Market among 16 to 19 year olds*, Sheffield: Training Agency Research and Development Series (in press).

Simpson, S. (1993) 'Areas of Stress within Bradford District', Research Section, Chief Executive's Department: City of Bradford Metropolitan Council.

Sivanandan, A. (1982) *A Different Hunger: Writings on Black Resistance*, London: Pluto Press.

Smith, D. J. (1974) *Racial Disadvantage in Employment*, London: Political and Economic Planning.

Smith, D. J. (1981) *Unemployment and Racial Minorities*, London: Policy Studies Institute.

Smith, D. J. and Tomlinson, S. (1989) *The School Effect: A Study of Multi-Racial Comprehensives*, London: Policy Studies Institute.

Solomos, J. (1986) 'Varieties of Marxist conceptions of 'race', class and the state: a critical analysis', in J. Rex and D. Mason (eds.) *Theories of Race and Ethnic Relations*, Cambridge: Cambridge University Press.

Stanfield, J. and Dennis, R. (1993) *Race and Ethnicity in Research Methods*, London: Sage Publications.

Taylor, M. (1984) 'Growing up without work : a study of young unemployed people in the West Midlands', in *Growing up without work : Two Case Studies*, Maastricht, The Netherlands: European Centre for Work and Society, Studies and Document 4.

Taylor, M. J. (1981) *Caught Between: A review of Research into the Education of Pupils of West Indian Origin*, Windsor: National Foundation for Educational Research.

Taylor, M. J. with Hegarty, S. (1985) *The Best of Both Worlds ...? A Review of Research into the Education of Pupils of South Asian Origin*, Windsor: NFER-Nelson.

Taylor, P. (1992) *Ethnic Group Data for University Entry*, ESRC Centre for Research in Ethnic Relations, University of Warwick.

Thomas, M. E. (1993) 'Race, Class and Personal Income: An empirical test of the declining significance of race thesis, 1968-1998', *Social Problems,* , Vol 40, No.3, 328-342.

Times Educational Supplement (1984) Blacks 'more choosy' about jobs, TES, 7.9.84.

Tizard, B., Blatchford, P. Burke, J., Farquhar, C. and Plewis, I. (1988) *Young Children at School in the Inner City*, London: Lawrence Erlbaum Associates.

Tomaskovic-Devey, D. (1992) 'How come everybody looks like me? The sources of job level, sex and race segregation'. Paper presented at the International Sociological Association Research Committee International Conference, University of Trento, Italy, 14-16 May.

Tomlinson, S. (1983) *Ethnic Minorities in British Schools: A review of the literature 1960-81*, London: Policy Studies Institute.

Tomlinson, S. (1987) 'Curriculum Option Choices in Multi-ethnic Schools', in B. Troyna (ed.) *Racial Inequality in Education*, London: Tavistock Press.

Tomlinson, S. (1991) 'Reports: Education and training', *New Community*, 18(1): 133-139.

Troyna, B. (1984) 'Fact or Artefact? The "Educational Under Achievement" of Black Pupils', *British Journal of Sociology of Education*, 5 (2).

Troyna, B. (1992) 'Can you see the join? An historical analysis of multicultural and anti-racist education policies', in D Gill, B

Mayor and M Blair (eds.) *Racism and Education*, Sage Publications, pp. 63-91.

Troyna, B. and Smith, D. (1983) *Racism, School and the Labour Market*, Leicester: National Youth Bureau.

Troyna, B. and Williams, J. (1986) *Racism, Education and the State*, London: Croom Helm.

Ullah, P. (1985) 'Disaffected black and white youth: the role of unemployment duration and perceived job discrimination', *Ethnic and Racial Studies*, 8, 2.

Ullah, P., Banks, M. and Warr, P. (1985) 'Social support, social pressures and psychological distress during unemployment', *Psychological Medicine*, 18:283-295.

Verma, G. K. and Darby, D. (1987) *Race, Training and Employment*, Lewes: Falmer Press.

Whitfield, K. and Bourlakis, C. (1989) *YTS and the Labour Queue*, Sheffield: Employment Department Training Research and Development Series, No. 54 - Youth Cohort Series No. 8 (pp. 23).

Willis, P.E. (1977) *Learning to labour: How Working Class Kids get Working Class Jobs*, Farnborough, Hants: Saxon House.

Wilson, A, (1987) *The Truly Disadvantaged*, Chicago: the University of Chicago Press.

Wrench, J. (1993) 'Reports: Employment and the labour market', *New Community*, 19(2): 311-317.

Wrench, J. and Lee, G. (1983) 'A subtle hammering - young black people and the labour market', in B. Troyna and D. Smith (eds.) *Racism, School and the Labour Market*, Leicester: National Youth Bureau.

Young, K. (1992) 'Approaches to policy development in the field of equal opportunities', in P Braham et al (eds.) *Racism and Anti-Racism: Inequalities, Opportunities and Policies*, London: Sage Publications, pp. 252-269.

Zegers de Beijl, R. (1991) *Although Equal Before the Law: The Scope of Anti-Discrimination Legislation and its Effects on Labour Market Discrimination Against Migrant Workers in the UK, The Netherlands and Sweden*, Geneva: International Labour Office Working Paper.

Subject index

differential non response, 66
direct discrimination, 164, 187
discouraged worker, 50, 101
discrimination, 8, 14, 132

economic activity rate, 49, 71
economically inactive, 70
educational achievement, 21
equal opportunities, 145
equal opportunities policies, 9, 178
equality of opportunity, 14
equality targets, 10, 192
ethnic minorities, 62
Ethnic Minority Grant, 192
ethnic monitoring, 11, 192
ethnic penalties, 189
ethnic question, 61
examination achievement, 60
examination results, 15, 74

family background, 70
family size, 164
formal investigations, 9
further education, 90

gender, 14, 17, 75, 87, 92, 100, 109, 125, 132, 144, 157, 163, 179, 183, 186, 191
gender differences, 92
geographical areas, 24
Germany, 12
government policies, 192

harassment, 5
health, 187
higher education, 15, 89
higher grade passes, 81
home background, 70
housing, 33, 187
housing tenure, 71

human capital theory, 51

ILEA, 25, 29
immigration, 8
independent schools, 69
indirect discrimination, 164, 189
inequalities, 132
inner city, 179
institutional racism, 12
integration, 4
Internet, 187
IQ, 6
ITEC, 45

Labour Force Survey, 33, 66
Lewisham, 38
linguistic needs, 4
Liverpool, 38, 45, 46, 138
local labour market, 46, 133, 185
logit analysis, 38, 163, 165
logit modelling, 178
logit models, 68, 100, 133
long term unemployment, 185
low income, 100

Manchester, 50
Manpower Services Commission, 39
manual jobs, 49
manual occupations, 186
manufacturing, 178
manufacturing industry, 50
marital status, 164
Marxism, 19
Metropolitan Police, 18
mother's occupation, 63
multi cultural, 7
multi cultural issues, 7
multi level analyses, 193
multi level model, 164

Author index

212